CHAMELEON
Confessions of a Former
People-Pleaser

CHAMELEON
Confessions of a Former People-Pleaser

Rebecca Weller

Mod By Dom ~ Australia

CHAMELEON
Confessions of a Former People-Pleaser

Cover and Interior Design by Dominic Garczynski.
Cover photography by Royden Monteiro.

Paperback ISBN: 9780994602374
Digital ISBN: 9780994602367

ModByDom.com

For anyone who has ever abandoned themselves.
I wish you the magic and joy of finding
your way back to yourself.

And for my Nan, Thelma, who always saw the
best in me, even when I didn't see it in myself.
Thank you for teaching me how to lead with love.

Contents

1. The Original People Pleaser

It's often said that wedding planning can be stressful and has the ability to create the kind of Bridezilla that would make a sailor blush. But for a full blown people-pleaser? *Oh boy.* It can be a living nightmare.

I was thirty-one the first time I walked down the aisle, which sounds like an age when a woman should know exactly who she is and what she wants. To be honest, I thought I did. After all, it was me who pressured my boyfriend to hurry up and propose. *("Hello! The clock is ticking. What are we waiting for? I don't want wrinkles on my wedding day!" Charmed to meet you, I'm sure.)* It was me who organised a big, elaborate wedding, all by myself. And it was me who spent the morning after the wedding sobbing so hard in the shower I could barely breathe.

I wasn't upset about the man I'd married. I really did love him. But I was a confused jumble of hurt, resentment, frustration, and bone-crushing *depletion*. And I really didn't understand why.

It had all seemed like such a brilliant plan. My then-fiancé, Luke, and I had only recently made the cross-country move from Sydney to Perth. Since his family lived overseas, mine lived more than 400km out of the city, and the vast majority of our friends lived interstate, I dreamt up the spectacular idea to book out an entire resort for two nights. Everyone seemed thrilled with the idea, and I was so excited about the thought of staying and playing together for longer. The resort had three pubs on site, so I imagined us all whooping it up the entire time; one long, never-ending party, just the way I liked it back then.

Oh sure, it would require magician-like skills in logistics to manage a group booking and be a stellar hostess for the whole weekend, but I was up for the challenge. I'd always been a big Planner with a capital P, and this was the perfect project for me to really sink my teeth into. Plus, I had almost an entire year to organise everything. *What could possibly go wrong?*

We'd agreed to keep the guest list fairly small (we were paying for it ourselves, after all), but that didn't mean I couldn't ensure every touch was just perfect for our eighty or so favourite people. Doing everything myself would also do wonderful things for our budget, of course. Not only would I be an epic planner; I'd also be a savvy spreadsheeting *genius!*

In the months leading up to the big day, I was an intense whirlwind of productivity. It was 2006, and Pinterest hadn't yet been invented, but don't you worry; I devoured every bridal magazine I could get my hands on, cover to cover. I spent a small fortune on those glossy, seductive pages and believed every single word when they said that a proper wedding involves a checklist of 138 absolutely essential tasks, none of which could be skipped *or so you help you,* the heavens would rain a *monsoon* down upon your wedding day!

Naturally, I agonised over the guest list, horrified by the thought of forgetting or upsetting anyone. A few of our closest friends insisted that a cocktail-style reception was always the best fun for mingling and partying. Truth be told, I figured it would also be a very convenient way to avoid any complaints about the seating arrangements, so that was the style we booked, even though part of me really wanted a sit-down dinner.

Once I got the planning-ball rolling, my fiancé was sweet and let me run with it. He didn't help me with the massive workload, but then again, I didn't ask him to, either. I was just so happy to finally have a diamond ring on my finger. He'd done his part. I could take it from there.

Determined to make everything from scratch and ensure every single element was just perfect, I spent endless nights frantically gluing sparkly hearts and ribbons to our invitations, and countless weekends trawling vintage stores, searching high and low for darling little candles and vintage vases to create the most exquisite decor. Our living room floor was covered in enough glitter to choke a unicorn, and our spare bedroom was crammed with so many candles, polyester veils, and paper gift bags, it was practically a bomboniere bonfire waiting to happen.

Somewhere in amongst this flurry of activity, I figured I didn't *quite* have enough on my plate, and my fiancé and I decided we should also buy a block of land and build a house. *Because, why not!* We still had five months to go until the wedding, after all. Surely that was plenty of time to drive all over the city to look at land, organise a mortgage, enlist a building company, apply to council for approvals, and make the four thousand other decisions that go into choosing every single element for a new house? Other people did that while wedding planning, right?

I still had the Hens and Bucks parties to organise as well, of course. I hadn't forgotten about those. Since our bridesmaid and best man lived interstate and overseas, they wouldn't be able to organise them for us.

Many of our friends and family could only take time off work over the Christmas and New Year holidays, so we'd chosen January 4th as our wedding date, which meant all of our festivities had to be squeezed into those few precious days. But nothing was a problem! *I was a solution-savvy Queen!* Not only would these be the most amazing Hens and Bucks parties our guests had ever flown in for - and all take place within the very same week as our wedding - but I'd even throw in a big New Years Eve party at our place and really knock their socks off. *Viva la celebration!*

I was holding it together. I really was. But when my fiancé invited a couple of his friends to stay with us in the days leading up to the wedding, my stomach churned. For one, it meant I'd have to find some-where else to store everything I'd shoved into the spare bedroom. For another, it meant finding room for their baby who'd need a quiet place to sleep. Our home was tiny, and I had a sneaking suspicion that things were going to be super hectic in those final few days. Against my better judgement, even though I really didn't want them to, I agreed. I hated the thought of disappointing anyone, and my poor little anxious bunny heart didn't know how to say no.

After that? Well, it was on for young and old. As word got out, other friends and family asked if they could borrow our car, or extend their trip and take our spare bedroom as soon as it was vacant, which meant I also felt pressured to organise extra sets of keys, clean the sheets, and restock the fridge.

My fiancé was as generous and unable to say no as I was, which meant the 'yes' parade kept marching on. Just when I thought we'd accommodated everyone, yet one more friend chimed in with a couch surfing request and a pitiful, "Well, if they're all staying, can I stay too?"

Inside, I was growing perilously close to meltdown status, but instead, I nodded and mumbled yes.

SURE, Craig, you and your twenty-eight siblings can come stay with us. Oh, you wanna bring your cat too? No problem! Take our bed; we don't even sleep!

Meanwhile, not only was I frantically trying to organise all of the wedding details, but I was also tearing my hair out helping everyone book their flights and accommodation at the resort. Of course they could do it themselves, but everyone knew I was great at organising, so what was the harm?

Hell-bent on ensuring everyone had the smoothest travel plans ever, I made myself completely available at all hours of the day and night. Which meant that instead of asking the resort their questions, they asked me.

"Hey Bex, does our room have an interconnecting door? We want to be close to so-and-so."

"Does our room come with a hairdryer or do I need to bring one from home? Or better yet, do you think you could bring yours for me to borrow?"

"Do they have any dairy-free options on the breakfast menu? I'm not so good with lactose."

"Actually, could we swap rooms with so-and-so? We've decided we don't want to be right next to the pool after all."

In addition to the thirty-nine emails and phone calls I fielded each day from our wedding guests and suppliers, I was also took calls from our local council, bank, and building contractors. I was fuelled exclusively by coffee and sugar, and in such decision fatigue that everything had started to blend together: flowers, celebrants, cakes, taps, tiles, interest rates…

As our wedding date grew nearer, naturally the intensity only escalated. By this point, the weight of responsibility was suffocating me. *But these people were flying all this way!* I wanted to ensure that everyone had the best time and we were wonderful hosts. I wanted my fiancé to enjoy as much time with his loved ones as possible. And I certainly didn't want to complain or let anyone to know I was struggling.

The hard fact was, I didn't know how to ask for help, and I certainly didn't want to burden anyone else, or have them think I was a bother (or worse, a Bridez-illa!). I was a woman overboard and I was sinking fast, but it was too late now. I'd made my almost-marital bed, I was just going to have to keep up my agreeable, pleasant demeanour and save my breakdown until it was all over.

Unfortunately, the one place we can't hide from stress is within our own bodies.

I'd always envisioned waking up on my wedding day feeling like birds were chirping and angels were singing, just like I'd been promised in every romantic movie. Instead, I woke up feeling worse than I could ever remember. I very rarely got sick, and I certainly didn't have the bandwidth or patience for my body to give out on me so close to our nuptials, so I swallowed a ton of cold and flu tablets and marched determinedly on.

Turned out I wasn't the only one barely keeping it together. Mother Nature was clearly in the very same mood. A freak summer storm blew in, putting rest to my dream plan of getting married poolside, and instead resulting in a last-minute switch to one of the resort's corporate function rooms.

If I thought my job as Wedding Planner was finished when I walked down the aisle, I was sorely mistaken. During the reception, a family member came up to complain that there wasn't enough food and everyone was starving, and instead of asking her if she could take care of it, I tracked down the restaurant manager myself and begged her to bring out more cana-pés. Moments later, another friend tugged on my arm to let me know that our long-lost relative was drunk, and I took it upon myself to go pour some water into her. One of our guests handed me a phone and told me someone wanted to wish me congratulations, and instead of asking them to call back tomorrow when I no longer had a function room full of guests to host, I took the call.

When I finally felt like I'd done enough, I slid myself into a chair sometime around ten p.m.. I was so sick I could barely think straight, dizzy and dosed up on medication I'd washed down with champagne. A couple of friends noticed how unwell I looked and insisted that I go tell my fiancé I needed to lie down. Despite the fact that every bone in my body begged me to comply, I refused. "No. Look at him. He's having the best night of his life, bless him. And everyone's come all this way. I'm tough. I'll be fine."

When we finally left after midnight, we were sent

off amidst a beautiful chorus of "congratulations!" and a sea of requests for our time the next day.

Locking myself in the bathroom the next morning felt like escaping to my own private paradise. I was alone. It was over. At least for a moment, no one could find me, or reach me, or request this or that.

As I stepped into the shower and turned on the hot water, I couldn't hold it back any longer. Huge tears of relief and resentment rolled down my cheeks. I was horrified and ashamed to realise I was sick of everyone and everything! There were so many joyful and wonderful moments in amongst the 'workload' of the day, but I found it almost impossible to extract or enjoy them. I was too lost in the smothering sense of obligation and sheer exhaustion. I didn't feel elated, like I'd just experienced 'the best day of my life' - I felt relieved that the whole damn thing was over and I'd actually survived the process.

My reaction baffled me. I'd wanted this wedding for so long. I truly loved everyone who'd come to celebrate with us. *What was wrong with me?*

As I struggled to get a hold of myself, I cast my mind back to the very beginning. I didn't realise it at the time, but I'd totally bought into society's pressure and ideals around young people being 'left on the shelf' if they weren't married by thirty. I'd felt the pressure to be married closing in on me every day. I'd wanted to be chosen so badly. I wanted to feel loved, cherished and desired. I wanted the romance and the fairytale. Most of all, I'd wanted to be known as a wife; as a partner in something; as someone's special person.

Before I effectively bullied him into finally propos-
ing, it devastated me that my boyfriend was in no hurry
to walk down the aisle, even though we'd been living
together for three years. I mean, we were thirty years
old, already. *What was he waiting for?* More crucially,
what would people think?

As much as I tried to be happy for them, it
completely crushed me whenever yet another friend or
colleague announced their engagement. I felt sick with
envy whenever I received yet another wedding invitation in the mail. *Why wasn't it happening for me?*

At work, I really liked most of my colleagues, but
there was one guy in particular I always tried to avoid.
Unfortunately he seemed to have only three modes of
operation: rude, arrogant, or cringingly inappropriate.
I found him impossibly annoying, and yet, one day *he*
showed up wearing a new wedding band! It killed me
to know that someone had promised him forever.

Someone actually loved him enough to marry him!
Why didn't my boyfriend love me?

Forget loving myself; I wanted someone *else's* love.
My greatest fear was that people would see the absence
of a wedding ring on my finger and know that no one
in the world wanted me to be forever theirs. I conve-
niently forgot all about my first year in London and
how happy I was to be single after being in the wrong
relationship once before. All that drove me was the fear
that I was flawed and unlovable, and that not wearing a
ring meant everyone else could see it too.

My motivation - the energy underpinning the entire day - had been off from the very beginning. I didn't want a celebration of our love; I wanted a milestone achievement award that others would recognise. I wanted a big, elaborate wedding to show and prove to everyone else: *see how happy we are?*

I wanted to include all the things that people were expected to include in a wedding, so that I did it 'right' and it was 'perfect'. I rarely stopped to consider whether it was something that was actually aligned with our tastes and preferences.

Between trying to ensure I planned the perfect event, and worrying about what others would think about me not being married yet, I completely lost sight of what really mattered: the relationship and connection I shared with my fiancé.

I put everyone else first. I said yes to everything because, at its core, I wanted everyone to like me. I was convinced I was deathly allergic to conflict of any kind, so I bent over backwards to make sure everyone else was happy. I twisted myself into a pretzel to please everyone, and consistently made other people's needs more important than my own. I wasn't being honest, because more than my own authenticity and truth, I desperately wanted everyone else's approval.

The maddening thing is I did this all to *myself*. Other people didn't know they were wearing out their welcome, or asking too much of me, because I didn't make a peep. It was the fears and beliefs that lived in my head that caused all this; my inability to directly communicate and be open and up-front with others.

I was a people-pleaser, through and through.

My particular flavour was two scoops of loving doormat. A soft serve cone of spinelessness. It included being constantly agreeable and compliant. Taking on way too much. Morphing myself to fit in with the crowd. Never asking for help. Not speaking up or being honest about my true feelings. Having zero boundaries or communication skills. Struggling against an unholy fear of any type of conflict (including sheer panic at the mere hint of the words, "We need to talk"). Possessing a complete inability to say no when I so desperately didn't want to say yes. Obsessively worrying about what others thought of me. Handing control of my emotions over to other people. And above all, a danger-ous lack of self-trust, love, and self-worth.

People-pleasing is a pattern that often begins in our childhoods as a coping mechanism; a way to feel safe and loved. Perhaps you had a fairly happy childhood but were taught that you had to be 'good' in order to earn love and affection. Maybe you had parents who were too busy or stressed to have any patience left over for your emotions, so you learnt that your true feelings don't matter. Perhaps you had a parent who struggled with addiction or emotional volatility or some other kind of unhealed trauma, and you learnt it wasn't safe to speak up. It was vital to your survival to be good and quiet and perfect in order to avoid attracting attention to yourself, or to keep the peace. Or, it may have even been that your family moved around a lot and you found that being a chameleon was a fast and effective way to fall into new groups and make new friends.

Whatever circumstance brought you here, somewhere along the way you learnt to distrust and abandon yourself in order to be what other people wanted you to be. In your young and impressionable mind, being compliant and conflict-averse equalled safety, love, and approval.

I know, because my mind believed that too. It was a belief so deeply programmed into my subconscious that I had no idea it was still running the show (and my life) as an adult. It was evident in every corner of my overstuffed calendar, my constant state of near-burnout, and how traumatised I was any time I wanted to break up with someone because I was terrified of hurting him and disappointing everyone.

I was petrified of not being liked, of being a burden, of doing anything that might hurt somebody's feelings, and of the slightest confrontation. I continually prioritised being liked over being respected, and panicked when others seemed irritated or mad at me. All of which meant I was forever putting my own needs last and then feeling resentful that people couldn't read my mind. That resentment, of course, left me constantly searching for an escape hatch in the form of alcohol, sugar, shopping, dieting, or some other form of addictive self-destruction.

I was less interested in exploring who I was, and more interested in figuring out what others wanted me to be.

A massive transformation happened between that fateful wedding day and the day I walked down the aisle for the second time, and it wasn't only the difference between drinking and sobriety, my age, or the man I was marrying.

It's as though I finally woke up. I took the blinkers off, and slowly, painfully grew up. I learnt to speak up, tell the truth, and ask for what I need. I discovered that everything I'd always needed was already inside of me, including - and especially - the love and validation I so desperately craved.

Far from being the scary, confronting place I thought it'd be, that new place of emotional health and maturity felt glorious. It felt blissfully liberating after so many years shape-shifting in order to please others.

It felt like a revelation after a lifetime of betraying myself.

2. Our Deepest Fear

When I was little, my grandmother would often call me 'magpie', because wherever we went, I was fascinated by shiny objects. There was something just so lovely about sparkles, shiny metals, and coloured stones. Although I was way too busy trying to be 'good' to ever steal anything (unlike the European folklore of the bird), whenever we went to a garage sale or local market, Nan laughed as she watched me become entirely enchanted by whatever trinkets or vintage jewellery were on display.

Silver was my favourite, and over the years, although I didn't buy a large amount of it, I could never bear to part with any of it either. Which landed me, in my mid-forties, with thirty-odd years worth of silver necklaces, rings, bangles and earrings.

"What's all *this* stuff?", asked my husband, Dominic, looking thoroughly puzzled as he pulled a loaded bowl from one of our lower kitchen cabinets one day.

"My old jewellery," I informed him, as though that explained everything.

"*Okayyy*," he said, looking straight at me and then glancing back at the bowl in his hand. "So what's it doing in *here?*"

"Well…" I said, blushing and attempting to shrug it off. "I don't really like it anymore, and it's all tarnished."

In truth, I'd stashed it there so I wouldn't have to think about it, and certainly wouldn't have to make any decisions about it.

Dom laughed out loud. "Well, then, why do we *have* it?"

As I attempted to think of a reason that might sound halfway logical, he placed the bowl down on the bench and started sifting through it. "What is it all, anyway? Why don't you like it?"

"I mean… I guess some were gifts that don't really have great memories attached to them, some were travel souvenirs, or little celebration presents I bought myself. But it all kind of feels like a big reminder of the Old Bex, you know?"

By that I meant pre-sobriety Bex. Pre-self-aware Bex. The people-pleasing, clueless and lost Bex. There was so much heavy energy tied up in those memories, which was precisely why I'd hidden it all under the sink in the first place.

"So let's clear it out," Dom shrugged.

"Okay," I nodded, biting my lip. "I just need to clean it first."

I didn't, really. Whether I ended up selling or donating it, I really didn't have to go to the trouble of doing anything with it first. I was stalling for time, although I had no idea why.

"Okay, so let's do that." Dom stared at me for a few beats before I realised he meant right this minute.

"Like, *now?*", I checked, thrown totally off guard.

"What are we waiting for?", he laughed.

Nodding, I headed off to rummage around in the laundry cupboard until I found the silver cleaner, and we spent the next hour cleaning and polishing off decades of tarnish.

"Done!" Dom said when we'd finally finished the lot. "Okay, let's go take it somewhere now. I'll get the keys."

"Oh, hang on." I reached out to stop him. "We should just… maybe let it all settle first. Maybe even give them another once-over tomorrow."

Dom looked at me with all the confusion I felt. "*What?* Why?"

It was a perfectly reasonable question. I glanced down at the pieces given to me by ex-boyfriends that only made me feel terrible. Each one held a painful reminder of all the ways I'd messed up in those relationships; all the ways I'd pulled away and behaved in ways that had caused them to lose respect for me. Usually they were buried deep in the back of the cupboard where I wouldn't have to see them and be reminded. I didn't like seeing them. And yet, for some baffling reason, I was still rallying against letting go.

"*Ugh,*" I groaned dramatically, so darn sick of the internal agonising and hand-wringing. I desperately wanted to box it all back up and just think about it later. Instead, I started processing my thoughts out loud. "I don't wear it, or even *like* it any more, but… I don't know… I feel like I want to, but I don't know if I should…"

"What's the problem?" Dom said, clearly growing frustrated. "It's not like you're never, ever going to have access to jewellery ever again in your life. *I will buy you jewellery!*" He teased me with a cheeky grin.

"I know, I know," I nodded, managing a weak smile. I knew I was being completely weird and unreasonable. I could easily buy my own jewellery, too. It was only silver; it wasn't expensive.

As I started packing it all away again, and Dom headed off to focus on something else, I desperately struggled to make sense of the hot, tight sensation in my chest. In a daze, I walked around the house, mulling it over. I was stunned to find myself close to tears, and found the whole saga utterly baffling. *What on earth was wrong with me?*

Suddenly, in a blinding flash, it hit me. *Praise the heavens above,* I recognised the emotion. It was just big old fear, that's what. Fear of letting go of the past. Fear of a future that held no guarantees.

Sheepishly, I approached Dom again. "Okay, I

think I know what it is," I said.

"Mhmm?", he said, raising an eyebrow with a bemused look on his face, waiting for me to go on.

"Okay." I paused to take a deep breath, hoping it would come out right. "It's like… I don't want any of this stuff, but then there's this part of me that thinks… well… what if we break up and I never find anyone again, and I end up old and alone and hopeless at dating, and I forget I was ever loveable or that I was once a woman that men bought jewellery for?"

Dom was silent for a moment as he stared at me. "Wow," he said finally, a smile playing at the corners of his mouth.

"I know," I said, pulling a face before I started to laugh. Hearing it all out loud only highlighted the absurdity of it all. I was six years sober by that point and had done enough inner work to know that no-one else could ever have any real bearing on my self-worth unless I chose to let them. That I, more than anyone else, held the keys to my own happiness. And yet, this fear was still clearly running the show in my subconscious.

It wasn't about the material items. It was about what those objects stood for. Just like the tortured souls on the 'hoarder' television shows who covet the junk and random objects clogging up their hallways. I was holding onto this jewellery that I didn't even like - pieces that only held painful memories - in an attempt to somehow protect myself from feeling unloveable. *Wow, indeed.*

I once listened to a podcast episode where the host, a clinical psychologist, talked about the deepest human fear. She said the one thing that lies beneath all our behaviours is the fear that we are unloveable. I'd never connected the dots before, but it was certainly at the root of my inability to let go of my old silver jewellery that day.

It was also underlying my reaction to a school dance when I was twelve, when I came home, closed my bedroom door, threw myself onto my bed, and sobbed like my heart would break.

I was so full of hope that night. I'd worn my cutest outfit and even some blue eyeshadow and sparkly cherry lip gloss. There was a boy - a veritable dream-boat named Cam - who always went out of his way to talk to me and jump into the seat next to mine whenever the teacher would let him get away with it.

A few weeks earlier, each student in our class was assigned a Secret Santa recipient to give small anonymous notes and hand-made gifts to, throughout the month of December. To my girlish delight, a friend told me that Cam had bribed another boy to trade names with him so he could be the one giving me the secret notes and gifts.

I was a hopeless romantic even back then, and I was sure this would be the night he asked me to dance, and maybe, just maybe, to be his girl.

He didn't, though. To my utter dismay and devastation, despite all the attention he'd lavished on me throughout the year, Cam spent the entire night flirt-

ing, laughing, and dancing with one of the most
confident girls in school.

As eager and desperate as I'm sure I looked, standing there awkwardly on the side of the dance floor
while I watched all the other kids pair up, not one
other boy asked me to dance either.

My little twelve year old heart was crushed. Why
I'd decided to make that night about boys and not
about just having silly fun with my girlfriends, I'll
never know, but there we were.

My Mum had to work that night so a friend's
parent dropped me home. It was already past my little
sister's bed time.

"Hey!" Our babysitter greeted me warmly as I
walked through the front door. "How was it?"

"Good," I mumbled, making a beeline for the safety
of my bedroom and praying I'd make it there before
I started sobbing and was asked to explain myself. As
I collapsed onto my bed, my chest ached with shame
and self-loathing. *Why didn't anyone want me?*

I also know it was this very fear underlying the
obsession with my body shape that started when I was
nineteen, when my boyfriend casually told me about a
conversation he'd just had with a friend.

"And then Leo said Valentina's so much smaller
than his ex. And I said 'she's petite' and he said, yeah
man, my girlfriend's petite and I love it." My boyfriend
chuckled to himself at his brilliance. I'd just picked him
up from a city bar where they'd been drinking together
for a few hours, and you could tell.

"Oh?" I said, vaguely curious about what boys talked about when they were alone together, and particularly curious about whether or not my name had come up. "And what did you say?"

"I said my girlfriend's *voluptuous*." Grinning to himself, he started jabbering away about something else while my mind cranked into overdrive.

Valentina was one of my best friends. She was gorgeous and delicate and tiny, in direct contrast to my height. At five foot seven (and a half!) in flats, I was always so much taller than other girls, and I hated it. I hated standing out.

I didn't want to be voluptuous. It didn't occur to me for a second that this might be a good thing. It was the mid-1990's and Kate Moss and the 'heroin chic' waif look had well and truly descended. Monica and Rachel were already beginning to jostle for pole position as the thinnest *Friends* character, and every magazine screamed about The Zone, Atkins, and South Beach diets. I didn't know much, but I knew thin was good and fat was bad. I wanted to be petite too!

Translation in my subconscious? If I was thinner, people would love me more. So I did what, sadly, so many teenage girls do: I stopped eating. *I might never be petite as far as height, but I could damn well be petite in body size if only I applied myself.*

Needless to say, the next few years were torture. I started keeping a food diary and made challenges with myself to reduce the number of entries each day. Dizzy spells and almost fainting at work in the mornings became a regular occurrence as I delayed eating for as long as I could.

I lived with my boyfriend and two other flatmates at the time. Our bathroom scales lived in a third, spare bedroom, and every morning when I woke up, I tip-toed down the hallway to weigh myself. Often I closed my eyes and held my breath as I waited for the display to light up. If the number was lower than the previous day, *hallelujah!* I was in a great mood. If it was even a single gram higher, I was a mess, unable to think clearly about anything else.

As the weeks turned into months and I started receiving compliments from people about how slim I was looking, I became even stricter with myself. I cut out pictures of models from magazines and posted them in my diary as constant motivation and looked at them whenever I felt hungry. I also pinned these pictures up across one entire wall of the spare bedroom where the scales lived, as 'motivation'.

Looking back now, I'm surprised my flatmates didn't have me committed for my serial-killer-style 'wall of death', although no doubt they were either too smart or too scared to mess with me. I was moody, irrational, emotional, and completely obsessed.

By the time my body mass index (BMI) dropped to an unhealthy and dangerous seventeen, my boyfriend had had enough. He tried to talk sense into me but I'd started to feel a sick sort of power over myself. If I controlled my weight, I controlled my life (and my fears), right?

Meanwhile, ironically, my 'life' was also losing weight. I avoided eating out with friends or family because, well, that involved food. Activities I'd previously enjoyed became tainted by my anxiety around food, and friends pulled away as I became increasingly exhausted and snippy.

Sadly this went on until I was a nervous wreck. Even the smallest thing would cause me to burst into tears. It was affecting my relationships, my work, my study, and my sanity.

I was thin, but at what cost?

I did all of this in an attempt to fit in and make myself more attractive to other people; almost as though I had to convince or trick people into loving me. My own insecurity and lack of confidence were drivers, of course, as was putting too much stock into other people's words or opinions, but underneath it all was a desperate lack of self-love.

The first time I read the Stephen Chbosky quote, "We accept the love we think we deserve," a thunderbolt of recognition shot through me. It reminded me of something my friend Claire once said about her dating life. "It's like… the guys I like never like me back. And if they *do* like me, I think there's something wrong with them."

I knew exactly what she meant. When a guy told me he liked me, I was immediately looking for the place where his logic was flawed: where he'd made a mistake in finding me loveable. I instinctively flipped the script and focused my attention on *his* flaws because, deep down, I didn't feel worthy of anyone else's love. I didn't even have my own.

That stubborn, pesky fear of being unloveable was, of course, also there when I was thirty-one years old and breaking my neck to rush down the aisle. It was there in my drinking to excess. And it was this very same fear that drove my impulse to please other people.

I was a chameleon because I was endlessly trying to blend in in order to feel safe. I was completely willing to embody whatever expression of myself seemed the most appealing to the person I was trying to get close to. By doing this, I believed I could avoid conflict, rejection and abandonment, and gain people's love, affection and approval.

But again, I was way off. Pretending to be someone I'm not didn't make me more loveable: it made me a good actress. Any love that version of myself received wasn't the whole picture, because I wasn't allowing it to be.

Only loving myself made me more loveable. Whenever I was secure and happy - when I was kind to myself and gave myself permission to be who I really was - I was more fun and loving to be around; I was a better friend, daughter, sister, girlfriend, and colleague. It all started with me. It all started within.

It all starts within you too.

Feeling unloveable is a fear. It's a belief, not a fact. A belief can be challenged, and then changed.

Loving yourself starts with acceptance of who you are and what makes you beautifully human, with all of your unique gifts, talents, quirks and foibles. When we shape shift and people-please in order to fit in and be loved and accepted, our relationships will never feel fulfilling because their entire premise is built on quicksand. They don't feel real because they're not built on authenticity. Being a chameleon means we risk feeling like no-one ever really *sees* us.

The only way to feel genuinely loved and accepted is to be your true self. Yes (deep breath), even if that means some people decide you're 'too much' or 'not enough'. You don't owe anyone a watered down or beefed up version of yourself.

You owe it to yourself to love and embrace who you truly are. This life is too short for anything else.

3. Fitting Out

In the Autumn of 2017, Dominic and I were nominated for a prestigious business award for our work helping women to live alcohol-free. Naturally, we were surprised and thrilled, and with bated breath, we waited weeks to find out if we'd made it to the next level. When the judges called to tell us we'd made it into the finals, we were absolutely beside ourselves.

Part of the process involved a site visit from the judges which, of course, was fine and dandy for those small businesses that had an actual, you know, office or official premises. We worked from home in our tiny city apartment. Dom had a small desk in the living room, while I worked from my equally pocket-sized desk in the second bedroom. We had zero other tables in the apartment; meeting, dining, or otherwise.

At first we figured it didn't matter, imagining it'd be like a little social chat. I pictured us perched on the couch with cups of tea, and how the judges would find our tiny home and big hospitality charming. I daydreamed about how fun it was going to be, and made a list of things to organise for that day, like an impressive variety of herbal tea, sparkling water served in pretty glasses, and delicious little bite-sized snacks.

Then the formal details of the site visit rolled in. Each company was assigned a different set of judges. Our email advised we'd be meeting with two Executive Directors of the company hosting the awards. Directors who'd accumulated more accomplishments in their long and sparkling careers than we'd had hot dinners.

"Fuck," Dom breathed as I finished reading their resumes aloud to him, and reality began to set in.

I stared back at him, dumbstruck, all images of bliss balls and pretty tea cups tap-dancing their way straight out of my naïve little head.

"Okay. Okay…" Dom said, pacing the living room and gesturing wildly. "Here's what we can do. Let's go talk to Yvette and see if we can borrow a table and some chairs." Our friend Yvette owned a nearby cafe. I furrowed my brow as I considered this zany idea.

"But… how would we get them here?" I asked. There was no way they'd fit in our tiny car.

"We'll carry them," Dom shrugged. The cafe was only two blocks away, but I really didn't fancy the idea of dragging a bunch of heavy chairs and table down the street like lunatics.

"But, hang on," I said, as something else occurred to me. "Would they even *fit* in here?"

"Yes," Dom nodded firmly, although I could tell by the look on his face that he wasn't so sure.

As I looked around the room, Dom grabbed a nearby plant and photo frame and started arranging them on the floor. "Okay, here, let's measure it out."

I grabbed the miniature brass drum that we used as a coffee table and placed it where a chair could possibly sit, while Dom ran and got the airing rack from our laundry.

"Okay," he said, coming back with it. "This is about the size of the cafe tables."

As he placed the airing rack in the centre of the space and we stood back, it was blindingly clear. This setting was tiny and yet it completely swallowed the room. There'd barely be any room to even push the chairs out from the table.

Dom looked at me, deflated.

"It's okay," I said, reaching over from my awkward position to comfort him. "We can sit on the couch."

"No, we can't!" he snapped.

"Of course we can. Come on, you were happy with that plan before. What's changed?"

"We've got the ex-head of one of the most successful companies in the country coming to visit, that's what!"

We both looked around at the little menagerie of household items we'd arranged in front of us, before turning to look at each other and bursting out laughing. It was all so ludicrous.

"Okay, stuff it!" Dom said when we finally caught our breath. "Let's just own it!"

And so the decision was made. I scrapped my scrumptious snacks idea, and instead we planned a plethora of things we could show the judges at Dom's stand-up desk in the corner.

Yes, we were different, but we were damn well going to *own* it!

This simple mindset adjustment relieved our stress and helped us to feel empowered. When the big day finally came, we excitedly showed the judges the work we'd been doing, and didn't give a second thought to the fact that we didn't have a boardroom table.

That one little perception shift gave us the confidence to embrace what was unique about us, and actually enjoy the experience.

Think about your favourite book, magazine, podcast host, or singer. There's some element of uniqueness in them, right? Something that makes them feel special or different to all the other books and singers you've ever seen in the world. Heck, think about your favourite pizza shop. What do they do differently to everyone else? That particular aspect you love about them isn't a flaw; it's what makes you feel a deep affinity for them.

The same is true for all of us. It's not our ability to blend in or be the same as everyone else that makes us beautiful or special or interesting; it's our uniqueness.

When I was studying to become a Health Coach,

we covered a concept that completely captured my imagination. Author Joshua Rosenthal talked about how much time and energy we waste trying to conform with the rest of society rather than living with authenticity.

I loved this so much. The truth was, I'd spent the vast majority of my life terrified of being different. I'd channelled vast amounts of my precious energy and creativity into it. It was in the clothes I wore, the conversations I was reluctantly a part of, and the three drinks I needed just to get my butt out the door to a party.

At a time when I was beginning to enjoy eating and thinking in a way that was different to the mainstream, this concept of 'fitting out' rather than desperately trying to 'fit in' felt like a deep exhale; almost like a permission slip of sorts, relieving me of the need to pretend I was just like everybody else.

More recently, as Dom and I packed up our old, tiny apartment to move across town into the first home we ever bought together, I came across my high school yearbook. As I plonked myself down on the floor and flipped through the pages, I wondered why I hadn't simply allowed myself to have more fun back then. I was so busy trying to have the 'right' hairdo, or the popular shoes, or to know the cool songs.

So much time and energy wasted channelled into fitting in. So much *potential* squandered on trying to prove I was just like everyone else, instead of embracing and loving up what was unique about me.

Whenever I saw someone happy and confident, I'd want what she had. It wasn't about the particular notebook, skirt, or shoes - it was about what I thought they'd give me: the same happiness and confidence that seemed to light her up from within. That was what was underneath it all.

Savvy marketers know it's what drives most of our purchasing decisions: who we think we'll *become* once we have that thing. And what lies underneath that desire is the fear that we're not enough, just as we are.

I didn't feel like I was enough, just as I was. And I certainly didn't feel strong or worthy enough to shine in all my strange and wonderful glory.

When you stop to think about it, it's pretty silly that we still feel this peer pressure past the age of sixteen. How many things do we do just to try to fit in with people we may not even like to begin with?

When I first embarked on my original sobriety experiment, this was one thing that scared me witless. *What would people say? Would I still be invited anywhere? How the hell would I socialise without a drink in my hand?*

The times I was closest to giving up my hard-won sober status were the times that I saw groups of friends on Facebook going to parties or big, boozy events together. I really didn't want to drink, but apparently I still desperately wanted to fit in. I was willing to trade what I truly wanted (to live my life authentically and alcohol-free), simply to be the same as everyone else.

I know I'm not alone in this. I've heard from

countless beautiful souls who worry about how they'll continue to fit in with their current friendship circles when they stop drinking. Each message is filled with fear; each person more terrified than the last of being the odd one out.

It makes sense, really. As humans, we crave connection. We long to belong. We trick ourselves into believing we enjoy being radical individuals, when in actual fact, we're often crippled by worries of what other people think; of being different, or of somehow standing out.

It's a fear well worth exploring within ourselves, because if we're afraid of being different, we can be brilliantly adept at finding ways to sabotage ourselves and our intentions. We might 'accidentally' and expertly trip ourselves up so we can remain 'safe' in our current network of friends, family and peers. This is precisely why such expressions exist as: "You are the average of the five people you spend the most time with", "Show me your friends and I'll show you your future", and "You can tell a lot about a person by the company they keep."

But, here's the thing. You can spend the rest of your life trying to be like everyone else, or you can spend it being true to yourself.

This is your one precious life. At the end of it, will you wish you'd had the courage to live your life for yourself, rather than what others expected of you? On your deathbed, will you wish you'd done more to fit in? Will you look back and wish you'd sacrificed your authenticity attempting to be the same as every-one else? Or will you wish you'd let your freak flag fly: that you'd been true to yourself and followed your own heart?

Think about the last time you saw a bunch of people dance or perform, whether it was in-person or on a TV show. Who was your attention most drawn to? Who couldn't you tear your eyes away from? Was it the person doing everything perfectly, and blend-ing in seamlessly with everyone else? Or was it the one so caught up in their own joy, they couldn't help but beam it across the entire stage?

Being true to ourselves and owning all our unique quirks and dreams is not only more joyful for us, it's also a whole heap more fun and interesting to every-one else. After all, the world would be a pretty grey and boring place if we were all cookie cutter replicas of each other.

You are beautiful and interesting precisely *because* you are unique.

If you think about the people in your life, it's prob-ably clear to you that you love each one for different reasons. Perhaps you have a friend who totally cracks you up every single time without fail. Maybe you have a family member with a really interesting perspective on life who always helps you to see things in a new way, or a colleague who's super sensible and wise, and always gives great advice.

Now imagine that instead of their unique personal-ities and talents, these people were all exactly the same as each other. It'd be incredibly dull, don't you think?

The more emotionally healthy we become, the more we crave authenticity. We love it when the people in our lives are more themselves - we recognise and appreciate how beautiful it is - and yet we tend to disregard the value of the same thing in ourselves.

This fear of being unique or different can drive our people-pleasing to perilous new heights. It can rob us of experiencing a deeper, richer life, and hold us back from the people we actually want to be close to.

But it doesn't have to be this way. Who wants to fit in, anyway? You're an adult now and the CEO of your own life. Why not actively choose to fit out? Rebel against the norm. Sing your own tune. Celebrate the myriad of ways you're different.

There's so much freedom in embracing and appreciating your uniqueness. The more you do it, the more you discover just how liberating and empowering it is. You get to know yourself again and what makes you happy, even if it's the complete opposite of what you thought it would be. You find out who you really are, what makes you tick, and what lights you up.

And that, it turns out, is the very key to liberating yourself from the need to seek approval and permission from others, for good.

4. Your Sensitivity is your Strength

When I was in my mid-twenties, I lived in a big share house in London, primed with young travellers from around the world. One night, I spotted a friend I hadn't seen in a while. It was a midweek evening and she was at my house visiting another friend.

As per my usual habit, I'd gone to the pub after work so was already a few drinks in when I found her. As I screeched hello and babbled on and on about any and every random thought that popped into my head, I thought I was being warm and hilarious. Her face said otherwise.

"Bex," she said quietly, attempting to get me to stand still long enough to meet her gaze. "You're a much more sensitive friend when you're not drinking."

Huh? I didn't get it at the time. I think my exact response was scoffing rudely at her while pulling a face. Who wanted to be *sensitive?* Not me! I'd always been led to believe it was a negative thing.

Any time someone had called me sensitive, it was usually after they'd thrown a mildly insulting or passive aggressive comment in my direction. Whenever they said, "Oh you're so sensitive!", it was often accompanied by an eye roll and intended as a criticism implying I was either too emotional, took things too personally, or lacked a sense of humour. Or potentially, all three.

No wonder I didn't want anything to do with the concept. *Of course* I didn't want to be the one feeling hurt over there in the corner. I wanted to have a hide like a rhino and laugh it all off. I wanted to be like everyone else.

It took half a lifetime, but boy, do I get it now. Hang out with anyone who's had a few too many drinks and see how much genuine kindness and empathy you get. Not much, right? They're on another dimension; a different plane of consciousness. As a result, your interaction with them is superficial; it's not real.

True sensitivity means not only feeling things more deeply, but also the ability to be more sensitive to the needs of others, including being wonderfully thoughtful, considerate, compassionate, and understanding. The ability to pick up on the feelings of others, to empathise and put ourselves in another person's shoes, is a rich and beautiful human quality. The world is a much warmer, kinder place for it. This trait becomes problematic only when we sacrifice ourselves for others, or attempt to deny our true nature.

For more than two decades, I leaned into alcohol as a way of escaping my sensitivity. I believed it was a burden; a personality flaw. I considered over-drinking a convenient way to cure my over-thinking. I thought booze made me confident and ballsy and resilient.

I was wrong. It simply denied my true nature. It simply meant I did a damn good job of shoving away who I really am.

When I stopped drinking and emerged from my hazy cocoon, suddenly I felt *everything*. Every struggle; every natural disaster; every injustice; every plight.

Suffice to say, *oh-my-word,* it was a lot.

Dom would often find me sobbing and I'd be completely unable to tell him why. "What's *happening?* Use your words!", he'd implore me, but I could barely even *understand* my emotions, never mind articulate the deluge that insisted on raining down upon my head. So many of these emotions felt completely new and foreign; I'd spent so long shoving them down or avoiding them completely.

Those first few months of sobriety were intense and exhausting, but they also forced me to realise that the sensitive, introverted, overthinking soul that had lived within me for the first sixteen years of my life was still very much alive. And that perhaps I had a lot to learn about embracing and making peace with her.

So many women I've had the honour of helping

have confided they also recognise or have rediscovered this sensitivity within themselves. Maybe you feel it too.

We tend to think of sensitivity - the ability to feel things very deeply - as a problem, because of other people's judgement, or because we confuse it with taking things personally. We might also judge *ourselves* for it, simultaneously feeling like we're too much and not enough. We might push this trait away because it feels like life is too intense, and we don't know how to navigate our emotions.

This was certainly why I was so quick to drink my sensitivity away; to numb the harsh realities of a world that felt 'too much'. Ironically, it was sobriety that not only reintroduced me to my sensitivity but also showed me that it's actually an incredible gift.

I mean, think about it for a moment. Didn't so many of the greatest paintings and music and books and films in the world come about because their artist was 'too sensitive'? These special souls had the ability to tap into emotions that others couldn't access. They felt everything ache deep in their bones, and could channel those intense emotions into something that makes the world more beautiful - something that helps others to understand and process their own emotions; that makes life more bearable; that signals understanding, love, and hope.

As my friend was so tactfully trying to tell me back in London, this sensitivity also has the ability to bring us closer to the people we care about. It makes us capable of not only greater empathy and creativity, but also deeper intimacy. It can actually strengthen our relationships - if we let it - including our relationship with ourselves.

When we deny our sensitivity, we not only cut ourselves off from our own emotions, we also reject an important part of ourselves that can serve as a crucial guidepost: our intuition. This is precisely what kept me stuck in a loop of chameleon madness for so long. I ignored my body when it sent me warning signs that I need to take a break, or that something (or someone) wasn't good for me. I believed that I owed other people superhuman strength, and I kept pushing through and overriding my natural instincts. I completely disregarded the inherent value of self-trust.

The more I did this, of course, the more I looked to others for answers rather than turning within and trusting my own inner wisdom. And the more I looked to others for guidance, the more I lost sight of myself.

It was only when I embraced my sensitivity, introversion, and overthinking (and began to think of them as real life superpowers!), that I finally felt at peace with them. I finally felt free to guide myself through life, and stopped being so very afraid of my own emotions.

Early one morning a few years ago, Dom and I took ourselves to the cinema for a date. I always love the first movie session of the day; the seats and floors are clean, the popcorn's hot and fresh, and if you're lucky, you might even find you have the entire cinema to yourself.

After much deliberation, we'd decided on a science fiction flick. We were both excited and happy, so as we settled into our comfy seats and the lights went down, I certainly didn't expect what came next.

In a single moment, completely without warning, hot tears stung the back of my eyelids and began to dribble down my cheeks. I was crying.

This flood of emotion wasn't in the middle of the movie like a normal person, *ohhhh* no. I cried about ten seconds into the trailer for an upcoming movie about a dog.

Another time, I was scrolling through my social media feed when I came across a friend's post recommending a television show. Curious, I clicked on the link to watch the season preview. As the little video played out, and the trailer showed lonely, elderly people joyfully bonding and connecting with four-year-old children, it happened again. I found myself silently sobbing.

Yes, my friend, apparently this is what I do now. *Pass the tissues, please.*

Sometimes it's a random act of kindness that invites the tears. Sometimes it's feeling deep empathy and compassion for the heartache that someone else is going through. Sometimes it's a movie trailer about a dog.

In the past, being sensitive or so quick to be moved to tears (especially in public!) would have embarrassed me no end. Now I'm incredibly grateful that I'm not flippant or numb to feeling deep empathy and emotion. I feel like I'm living and connecting more deeply because of it; not simply rushing through life focused on the surface level or minutia, but actually sensitive enough to really *feel* the full spectrum of human emotions.

It makes sense, really, that I was once terrified of my own sensitivity and emotions; it's innate in all of us. As humans, we're hard wired to want to avoid pain and move towards pleasure. Any time I didn't want to deal with emotions, I switched on the TV, ate more junk food, went shopping, or drank more wine.

Feeling anxiety? *Shove another chocolate in your mouth.* Having a stressful week at work? *Crack open another bottle.*

But all those years I was so willing and able to numb myself to the intensity of life, I was in fact doing myself a great disservice. As Brené Brown so wisely said: "We cannot selectively numb emotions. When we numb the painful emotions, we also numb the positive emotions."

One day more recently, Dom and I were walking in our local park when we started chuckling at a small, fluffy black dog who was having the time of his life splashing around in a puddle. At that exact moment, the dog looked up from his play time and spotted us. In a split second, his entire face lit up with unbridled joy, and he sprinted directly towards us like he'd been waiting for us his entire life.

There was so much pure love and joy in his tiny face and in this unexpected interaction that I couldn't help it. As I reached down to pat him, I completely welled up. Even just remembering the look on his face gets me all choked up again.

I know, I know, you guys. I really need to get my own dog.

My point is that emotions are incredibly beautiful. Painful? Yes. Scary? Sometimes. But always, always beautiful. They're proof of our depth, and the very thing that makes us most human. And we have the choice to run from them, or to embrace them.

Sometimes the depth of positive emotions I feel now stun me; so much so that I can't believe I ever wanted to numb out or hide from that kind of bliss. Those moments feels too exquisite; too precious to ever dilute or dampen down. Which always reminds me of famed poet, Mary Oliver, who summed it up when she wrote: *"Are you Breathing Just A Little and Calling it a Life?"*

The thing is, we all have our bad days. Deep or negative emotions are normal. They're nothing to be ashamed of. It's okay to weep at a movie, or lose your temper once in a while. Cry, scream under water or into your pillow, throw a short tantrum, let it all out. But don't spend your life running from who you truly are for the sake of an uncomfortable emotion. And don't beat yourself up if learning to navigate your emotions takes some time and patience.

Maybe, like me, you discover that in order to feel at peace with your sensitivity, you need more quiet, reflective time after socialising, or more time immersed in nature. Perhaps you discover you feel best if you incorporate more self-care into your routine, learning what you need and taking your needs seriously.

Whatever you're going through, at any time in your life, I promise, numbing out won't help. Lean into your sensitivity and your emotions. They're leading you somewhere. They're crucial signals and messengers on your journey of growth and evolution.

Don't let anyone judge you into feeling bad about this special gift you have. Embrace every last bit of it, including who you really are. When you feel things, you can change things. You can love and connect more deeply. You open the door to more joy and authenticity, for yourself and everyone around you.

Your sensitivity is your strength.

5. Release Your Expectations

Years ago, I travelled with a boyfriend to visit - and stay with - his family for the first time. Now, why on earth I thought it would be a good idea to stay in his parent's house the first time I met them, rather than *ohhh,* you know, actually getting to know each other first, I'll never know. But there we were; my boyfriend plus three perfect strangers, about to share a single bathroom for five days.

After we'd arrived and popped our bags in the spare room, we all sat down to get acquainted.

"Now, who'd like a coffee?" his Mum said, standing up and heading for the kitchen.

"Ooh, yes please!" I said, jumping up from the

couch to help her.

"No," she said, waving me away. "Sit! Sit!"

Nervous about making a good impression and desperate for them to like me, I did as I was told. It was only a couple of days later when I could see she was visibly knackered that I finally asserted myself, forcibly taking the tea towel from her hand and ushering her out of the kitchen so I could do the dishes.

As she complied, she turned to me and snapped, with sarcasm dripping from every word: "Well, I don't know why you'd want to help with *this*. You haven't wanted to help with anything else!"

Shocked, I stared at her. The weight of expectation pulled at the tension between us. She'd clearly expected that I was showing up as an extra set of hands and would make myself more useful throughout the week. She hadn't communicated this to me, of course, or asked for my help in any way. Quite the opposite. I'd therefore inferred that she wanted me to behave as a guest. In my previous boyfriend's family, guests were expected to stay out of the kitchen and simply express how much they were enjoying everything.

Looking back, should I have been more pushy and insistent on helping, day after day, regardless of her insistence that she didn't want or need it? Maybe. But if she truly hadn't wanted my help, we could have just as easily fallen into conflict there.

Things were strained between us for a long time after that, and all because of our personal - completely mismatched and misaligned - expectations, together with a lack of clear communication.

Aaahh, expectations. I remember the first time I read Anne Lamott's quote, "Expectations are resentments under construction." The penny echoed around in my head for a while before it finally dropped. I'd never stopped to consider exactly how many expectations I carried around with me all day long, about *everything.*

A friend should call back the same day! A family should want to have a big, happy Christmas together! A partner should just know when I'm upset, without me having to say anything.

The funny thing about expectations is they're rules for life that we either learnt during childhood, or made up in our own heads. And the funniest part is that each person is walking around with their *own,* potentially very *different* expectations.

We expect others to think exactly like us, but of course they don't. How could they? They weren't raised in our families; they haven't had the same relationships or life experiences. Their expectations are based solely on their own lives and the beliefs they've collected along the way. Just like ours. Expectations are completely biased and personal.

The worst part is that these expectations can get in the way of the very thing we want most. They can damage our relationships and become a self-perpetuating cycle. *Ask me how I know.*

Years ago, in a previous relationship, I had a boyfriend who wasn't really into the whole holidays and celebrations thing the way I was. Each Valentine's Day *(oh the heartache that day can cause!)* felt like a test of our love.

Every year I'd go to work and watch my colleagues receive flowers, gifts and cards. Each time they gushed about how wonderful and thoughtful their partner was, I'd feel a deep ache in the pit of my stomach, just knowing I was going to be disappointed. All day long I'd work myself into a state of despair, begging myself not to cry on the train home, telling myself that he'd have a romantic surprise waiting for me (like I did for him), but never truly believing it.

Once home, I'd walk through the front door, a veritable rain cloud of expectation and negative, tearful energy. Naturally, without me even saying a word, he could feel the weight of this expectation. We'd invariably get into an argument, and I'd spend the rest of the night sobbing.

Because of the heaviness of all of this - because of the weight of my expectation - he felt pressured and never quite good enough, so he continued to act that way. The whole mess became a vicious cycle that could so easily have been remedied by sitting down and talking honestly about it.

Perhaps his expectation was that once people were in a long-term relationship, they didn't have to do that kind of thing anymore, whereas back then my expectation was that the deeper you fell into love, the more you should show it. Perhaps, if we'd realised this, we could have come up with some kind of compromise we were both happy about. I could have ordered my own flowers and chocolates if that made me happy, and we could have had a low-key, casual dinner at home if that made him happy.

We'll never know, because neither of us had the emotional maturity or mental clarity to discuss it or ponder solutions. Instead, we argued, and drank, and then pretended the whole thing never happened. Until the next year.

The terrifying and ultimately beautiful thing I discovered about sobriety is that there's nowhere to hide. There's no numbing out or avoiding emotions or behaviours that are right in front of us. Slowly I began to see how my thoughts, beliefs and patterns drove my own behaviour. What I wanted most in that relationship was to feel loved, and yet my expectations only served to drive us further apart.

Although it can be gut-wrenching to admit, there's something incredibly empowering about taking responsibility for the energy *we* bring to the relationship. No longer do we feel like a victim. We begin to see solutions where there were none before.

Years ago I had a special yoga teacher. If I had to guess, I'd say she was in her sixties; possibly even seventies. Either way, she was infinitely more strong and flexible than I've *ever* been. As her class full of twenty and thirty-somethings sweatily attempted to recreate the pose she'd just demonstrated so effortlessly, she'd talk to us about *life* stuff.

One day she started talking about how we all spend

so much time in our heads 'social engineering' and constructing how we're going to tell someone about something that just happened to us, in order to get the reaction we expect.

I snapped my head up to look at her. *How did she know?* My mind had *just* been wandering, thinking about a little mishap earlier that day and how I was going to tell my friend about it in a way that would make her laugh the most.

As the teacher caught my eye and smiled, I felt a ripple of understanding. In my head, I already expected my friend to laugh with me. So how would I feel if she didn't? Disappointed? Annoyed? Upset?

Meanwhile, my friend may have had a busy day, her daughter might have gotten sick, or she might simply not have found the story (or me!) all that amusing. And yet, I was hinging my happiness on my own expectations. Expectations I'd created entirely in my own head.

Sadly, we can place all these expectations on ourselves as well. I once had a coaching client who sheepishly confided that she was terrified to stop drinking because she couldn't imagine not drinking champagne on her wedding day. This beautiful soul was single. She didn't even have a boyfriend yet, and *this* was the thing holding her back from experiencing sobriety.

The funny thing about this expectation; this rule for life that "she shalt drink champagne on her wedding day!", is that it was inherently flawed in a number of ways. Continuing to drink in the way she was might have kept her ideal partner away completely. If she *did* meet and fall in love with someone, who knows what he might be like. He might believe that a wedding is a sacred day about love and connection, and not want booze to be any part of it. Then again, she might discover how much she loves sobriety and find she doesn't even *want* alcohol on her wedding day. Or any other number of options!

We can all be guilty of this. We can allow expectations and romantic notions in our heads about the future, ruin our chance at happiness *today*.

If this concept is new to you, as it was to me, take a full day to digest this. Notice what triggers you and consider what it means about your expectations. Where did your expectations come from? How are they based on what's important to you?

Notice the moments when you'd really prefer that everyone thinks just like you, and times when you'd love to control other people's thoughts and actions.

Pretty wild, right?

Even more curious is the fact that we may bend over backwards to do things for the people in our life, based on what we *assume* they want or need. But unless we're born with some kind of superpower, we're not mind readers. Without impressive telepathic skills or clear communication, we have no idea what anyone else truly needs or wants. Furthermore, we have zero control over other people's reactions, heads and hearts.

As a recovering people-pleaser, I have to watch this.

Once, when I was about to travel over the Easter break, my then-boyfriend had to stay behind to work, so I came up with the fabulous idea to hide a bunch of chocolate Easter eggs all over our apartment.

For days, I hid little love notes with the chocolate gifts so that when I called him on Easter Sunday, I could send him on a treasure hunt. I was beside myself with glee with this idea, imagining how thrilled he'd be and how much it would totally brighten up his weekend, even though he had to work.

I could barely wait for that Sunday to arrive, and when it finally did, my grin almost split my face in two as I dialled his number.

When he answered, I could tell he was grumpy, but *don't you worry,* I knew just the thing to cheer him up!

"I've got a little surprise for you," I sang down the line, barely able to contain myself.

"Okay," he said wearily.

"Go to the laundry cupboard and look under the towels," I instructed him. I bit my lip as I waited, to stop myself from giggling. It was all so exciting! I was a flippin' Easter surprise *genius!*

"Okay," he said again as I heard him ruffling through the towels and opening the note.

"It's an Easter hunt!" I squealed. "I've hidden a bunch of gifts for you; just follow the notes."

I waited for him to laugh with delight.

And waited.

And waited.

Crickets chirped. Tumbleweeds rolled down the

street. The longest pause in history took place.

Figuring perhaps he didn't understand, I tried again. "They're presents. For you. To brighten up your weekend," I told him, speaking extra slowly so there was no chance of miscommunication this time.

"Uhhh, okay, thanks," he mumbled. "But that's enough, hey? No more."

Huh?

"Wh… what?" I stuttered, my heart falling through the floor. "What do you mean?"

"I mean I don't need any more presents," he sighed. "Okay, I've gotta' get to work. I'll talk to you later. Thanks though."

What the hell? I almost dropped the phone as I tried to comprehend what had just happened.

All that effort I'd gone to! I would have been *over-the-moon* thrilled if he'd done that for me. Why wasn't he *thrilled, dammit?!*

I'm sure you can imagine what came next. After I sobbed my eyes out, I became furious. How *dare* he not be excited and grateful!

I didn't know about Love Languages then, or even stop to consider that he might not see these kinds of gestures as my way of showing love. All I knew was that we were going to have one hell of a fight about this when I got home, *so help me God!*

Of course, I can see it now. The disappointment and ultimate resentment I felt were purely constructed by my own expectations. When I didn't get the reaction I was expecting, I was devastated.

But, here's the thing. People react in different ways for any number of reasons. When we hinge our peace of mind on other people's reactions, we put the key to our happiness in someone else's pocket.

Another time, after a friend casually mentioned she hadn't been able to find a cookbook she'd like to use for her upcoming dinner party, I ran all over town trying to find her a copy.

Okay, so she didn't specifically *ask* me to get it for her, but I imagined that maybe she was too polite, or too rushed, or too proud to ask for help. I was determined to come to the rescue. After all, that's what friends do! She wouldn't think I was a very good friend if I didn't act on it, now, would she?

Only, that damn book was sold out everywhere I looked.

After hours of searching, I finally located the darn thing, and when I triumphantly presented it to her, I completely expected her to throw her arms around me, crying tears of joy…

Instead, she shrugged and said, "Oh, okay, thanks. I actually didn't need it after all."

Gah!

The key to breaking this cycle is to practice awareness when I find myself doing it. Instead of getting carried away with my own assumptions and expectations, I can choose again. I can remain centred and simply open up the lines of communication with the people around me. I can gather more information and evidence before I run off half-cocked to 'help' or assist people who may not even need or appreciate it.

As for trying to guilt someone into giving us the reaction we want, *fuggedaboutit*. Repeat after me: *guilt destroys relationships.* Think about the last time you were guilted into something, or made to feel guilty about your reaction. Did it make you want to be closer to that person, or did it drive you emotionally further apart?

On the flip side, if you've ever been the recipient of a guilt apology, how did it feel? Disingenuous and empty, right? It makes sense. It was an apology given under duress, so it's never going to feel as sincere or as genuine as someone's true feelings.

This is not to say that you need to lower your expectations when it comes to other people's behaviour. You can (and absolutely should) still establish healthy boundaries and clearly communicate the kind of behaviour that is and isn't okay with you. It simply means not hinging your happiness on what others may say or do, and taking back control of your own happiness.

In other words, we can still do nice things for people, but it'll be so much better for our sanity if we do it simply because it makes us happy, without the strings of expectation attached.

The empowering part about all of this, is if our assumptions and expectations belong to us - if they live in our own heads - we can change them, anytime we like. We can choose to let go of the ones holding us back from living our best life, or damaging our chance at deeper relationships.

We can approach every preconceived notion with a valiant determination to get to the truth.

And the best part?

The more you release your expectations of others, the more you release other people's expectations of you. Permanently.

6. It Works Both Ways

Sometime in my mid-thirties, I went on a group holiday to tropical Bali. I was so excited about this trip. A bunch of my friends were flying in from all different places, and many of them had invited other friends to come along too. We planned to meet up and do a heap of different activities together throughout the week, culminating in a big party before we all flew home.

My people-pleasing was matched only by my binge drinking at the time, so I imagined us all having a whale of a time: one big, long, extended booze up. What I didn't imagine was that I'd almost immediately get what's known as 'Bali Belly': the infamous upset stomach also known as travellers' diarrhoea. Try as I might, I just couldn't tolerate alcohol in the way I'd planned.

Adjusting my expectations, I decided I'd just have to make the most of the trip and have as much fun as my body would allow during the daytime activities and head to bed early each night to try to sleep it off. Fingers crossed, I'd be all better by the night of the final party.

My plan worked for the most part. Provided I ate only plain food, drank mainly water, and took plenty of naps, I managed to keep it together. My friends gave me a lot of flack about not going out at night, but grudgingly forgave me as we had fun sunbathing, shopping, and sight-seeing throughout the week.

When the night of the party arrived, I felt a little better, but still not well enough to down an entire cocktail. Our hotel's pool bar had been transformed into a twinkling oasis. Lanterns hung from every wooden post, and the faint smell of frangipani flowers wafted by. The setting was every bit as beautiful as I'd imagined, but it was also an especially muggy, sticky night, and the humidity only deepened my lingering nausea.

Our group of friends were big drinkers and seasoned partiers, so it was all a whole lot louder (and sweatier) than I could handle sober, but by some miracle I managed to stay until midnight. I was incredibly proud of myself for making a huge effort to see the trip out with a bang, but also thoroughly exhausted and I couldn't wait to lie down and sleep in. I was flying out the next afternoon and was so looking forward to just relaxing by the pool on my final morning in total silence with a great book.

When a few people finally started to leave, I gratefully took it as my cue. On my way out, I bumped into a friend I hadn't seen in ages. I'd heard she was arriving in Bali that night and staying at another hotel, and that she might make it to the party.

To be honest, I'd kind of been dreading seeing her. We always had a great time hanging out (especially when I was drinking), but at the same time, I often found it hard to say no to her. Sometimes her requests came across as aggressive and I often found myself giving in simply because I didn't know how to stand up to her.

"Bex!" she squealed as she saw me, pulling me in for a hug. "Where are you going? Dance with me!"

"Oh, I can't hon; I'm knackered. I need to lie down." I smiled in apology. "Everyone else is still loving it, though. I hope you have a great night!"

"Whaaaat?!" Pulling me in so close that I could smell the rum on her breath, she said, "Okay, we'll do lunch tomorrow." It wasn't a question.

It was already well past midnight at this point and I was exhausted, physically and emotionally. I knew she was staying on for another week, while I was due to fly out the next afternoon. I'd been on the island - and actually feeling human - for such a short time. I really just wanted to soak up what was left of it, and not spend it traipsing all over the place trying to meet up with her.

"Oh," I said, completely caught off guard. "I leave at three tomorrow and plan to go from breakfast to a massage, so I think it'll be too rushed. We'll just have lunch when we get back home, huh?"

"No!" she insisted. "That's fine. We'll have lunch. There's plenty of time."

I stared at her for a beat before she demanded, *"Okay?"*

"Okay, we'll see," I said noncommittally, hugging her and making a hasty retreat.

Back in my hotel bed, I tossed and turned, wishing I didn't feel the crushing weight of her expectation all over me. The final party was *done*. I'd played my part and stayed until midnight so everyone would be happy. Now I just wanted a few hours to myself to finally relax, dammit!

Irritation and resentment simmered through me as soft dawn light peeked through the curtains. My body felt stiff and restless as I listened for the buzz of my phone; dreading her inevitable text message.

Suddenly, in a split second, something occurred to me.

Hang on! Why the heck was it always her way or the highway? What if I went back with a counter offer instead?

Thrilled and inspired, I reached for my phone and texted her. "Hey hon, I've got til 3pm before I need to shower and change for the airport, and I really want to spend it in my favourite pool! Wanna come over here for a swim and lunch?"

There! Done. The minute I sent the text, I felt the stress melt away. I was honest about my preference to stay exactly where I was, and offered an alternative way for us to spend time together that didn't involve me simply agreeing to meet her on *her* terms. More importantly, I hadn't betrayed myself by giving into pressure to do something I really didn't want to do.

When my phone buzzed with her reply a few minutes later, her message was filled with affection and even a slight apology. She wished she could, but later in the night she'd made plans with another friend, and she wanted to do that instead. And I felt completely at peace with it, because we were each doing exactly what felt right for us.

Later that morning on the massage table, I all but melted into a warm, gooey puddle of relief and relaxation all over the floor. All that angst and anxiety, when all I really needed to do was to follow my heart, take back ownership of my time, and be honest. Far from my fear that it would drive people away, it was another reminder that people tend to respect you more when you're honest about your thoughts, beliefs and preferences, even when they don't perfectly align with theirs.

When we're sensitive souls, one of our superpowers is that we're often quite adept at reading a room, which *can* be a good thing. This ability means we can temper our volume or vibrancy accordingly, and not stick our foot in it by celebrating our latest win at work when someone else has just been fired, or by announcing we just got a new kitten when someone else's beloved cat has just died. It means we have the capacity to be a more considerate friend, colleague, and human. Deep empathy allows us to be more tactful.

But one of the dangers of this is when we lose ourselves in this ability. When we mould ourselves to fit in with what we *think* other people want us to be, even going so far as to use other people's words, or say what we think they want to hear, we do so at our peril. When we're a chameleon in order to keep the peace, or keep everyone happy, we make other people's desires or preferences more important than our own.

More recently, a woman emailed me an invitation to an event she thought I should attend. I didn't know her, and she wasn't going to the event herself, but she was adamant that I should go. She thought it would be perfectly aligned with my interests and my work.

Although it was very kind of her to think of me, the event really wasn't my cup of tea. When I wrote back to thank her and politely declined, she pushed back with a big list of reasons why she insisted I should go.

In the past I would have gotten upset about this. I would have been furious at this person's nerve to presume they knew me well enough to pressure me into something. I would have felt suffocated under the weight of expectation, and quite possibly (maddeningly!), I would have even gone along to the event, simply to avoid the discomfort of disappointing her.

Instead, this time I thanked the Universe for giving me another opportunity to practice releasing the expectations of others. I chose to remember that I don't owe anyone my time or energy. My choices are mine alone, and every sticky or awkward situation provides me with yet another opportunity to grow, in both perspective and confidence.

I often think about what would happen if we were each born with a timer above our heads that counted down the amount of years, days, and hours we have left in our precious lifetime. Would we be so quick to give our time away? Would it help us to bring greater focus to the causes, people, and passions we care deeply about?

Because, let's face it. Timer or not, you can spend the rest of your life doing what others want you to do, or you can spend it doing what your heart yearns to do. This is *your* path, and your independence at stake. You don't have to feel pressured to do what family, friends, or perfect strangers think you should do. You don't have to lower your standards or act like a ninny in order to fit in with your friends. And you don't have to keep self small in an attempt to please others.

Of course, this doesn't mean taking free license to act like an asshole. It doesn't mean not caring about how you treat people, or not being a kind, caring, responsible human being. It simply means that your life belongs to you. All of it: your creativity, your career, your relationships.

One of my favourite artisan ceramics designers continues to be a huge inspiration to me in this area. A married couple who run a boutique studio together, they have a huge following online. Every couple of months or so, they launch a new collection of mugs and plates that sell out within minutes.

Each ceramic piece is splashed with colour in a unique way, so no two pieces are alike. Likewise, each collection has a different theme, so no two collections are alike. Which means if you miss out, you just have to cross your fingers and toes and hope you like what they do in their next collection (and maybe invest in a faster internet connection while you wait).

Whenever their fans beg them to make more of a certain colour or style, these artists unapologetically explain that because their creativity is incredibly important to them, they need to ensure they remain creatively inspired. This means boldly working on the next collection, even if some people are disappointed.

By remaining true to themselves rather than bowing to the expectations of others, they continue to feel fulfilled and inspired by their work, and can therefore continue to make beautiful art that is loved by people all over the world.

Letting go of all expectations relinquishes you of the need to betray yourself, or make yourself ill, trying to meet other people's requirements or desires.

It's not your job to live up to anyone else's 'rules for life', anymore than it's their job to live up to yours. It doesn't matter if your parents always expected you to go to university or have kids, or if your long lost friend expects you to be fully available to her every time she comes to town. You are only responsible for managing your own expectations, just as they are responsible for theirs. This is *your* life. They have their own.

7. It's Not Personal

A few months after my first book, *A Happier Hour*, was published, I was invited to take part in a long-form television program about Australian women and sobriety. The show's host and film crew flew across the country to interview both myself and a professor at a nearby university.

Deeming our apartment too small to film my interview, the show's producer hired a function room at a city hotel and asked me to meet them there. Knowing the story was for a high-profile show, I was all kinds of nervous, so Dom came with me for moral support.

After we arrived and made our introductions, the producer and the show's host immediately asked Dom to wait outside. Now that I know a bit more about how these interviews generally work, I realise we could have pushed back on that request and insisted he stay with me, but at the time we were both so green, we had no clue.

The film crew had switched off all the lights in the large function room, leaving most of the room in pitch black darkness. As I took my seat opposite the host, I could barely make him out just a few metres away. Bright portable studio lights shone directly onto me from all directions.

Before I'd left home, I'd meditated in an attempt to dispel my nerves.

The producer was lovely on the phone, I reminded myself. *Breathe like a normal person.* But it was no use; my palms were sweaty and my heart was racing. This was nothing like the dozens of podcast interviews I'd experienced. This felt more like an interrogation.

The host shuffled his papers and cleared his throat.

All you have to do is be honest, I told myself, taking another deep, shaky breath.

I was such a people-pleaser, though. *I mean, they'd come all this way. The least I could do was try to tell my story in a way they wanted me to.*

I attempted to relax but as the interview began, the host asked a string of peculiar, strangely worded questions that were completely different to the ones the producer had originally asked me over the phone.

Each time I answered one of the questions to the best of my abilities, the producer sprang over to whisper something in the host's ear and then ran back to her crouched position in the shadows.

In my attempt to be a 'good girl' and do what I was told, it didn't even occur to me to simply ask them to cut the crap and tell me which part of the story they wanted to hear, instead of being all cloak and dagger about it.

Finally, after what felt like hours of this nonsense, I sensed the interview was coming to a close. Taking another deep breath, I smoothed down my dress, giddy with relief to have survived the most bizarre interview I'd ever been part of.

"Now, before we wrap up," the host said, reaching into a bag beside him. "I have a gift for you!"

Oh, now *this* was a turn of events! How nice of them! I leaned forward in my chair, tapping my toes with excitement. I love fun surprises.

Reaching further into the bag, the host pulled something out. Through the alternating layers of darkness and blinding light, I couldn't quite make out what it was. It was only as he stood and reached across to hand it to me that I finally recognised the familiar shape.

It was a bottle of wine.

And now it was in my hands. *Huh?*

The lights, camera and microphone were still on me, but I couldn't help it. I cracked up laughing. It was all so ridiculous.

As the host sank back into his seat, I could see the disappointment spread across his face. This was clearly not the reaction he'd been hoping for.

"How do you feel, holding that?", he prompted,

presumably goading me for a bigger, different reaction. He was a *professional,* after all. He wasn't about to give up just because I'd laughed in his face.

I smiled and shrugged, saying the first word that came to me. "Free."

"Free?", he repeated blankly, darting a sideways glance at his producer.

"Yeah," I nodded, looking down at the bottle in my hands. "It's funny, because this used to be one of my favourites. But now, I feel nothing for it."

"Nothing at all?", he repeated slowly, waiting for something more. He glanced over towards his producer. They exchanged a meaningful nod before he turned back to me to ask, "Do you think alcohol is the devil?"

"No!" I laughed at his archaic choice of words. As I watched more disappointment spread across his face, I calmed myself enough to elaborate. "But now I see it for the cage it is, and I never want to go back there."

He nodded absently, as I stood and handed him back the bottle.

Weeks later, when the TV story finally came out, I wasn't overly surprised that it missed the mark completely. Nor was I overly surprised when a tabloid most well known for their scandalous drama republished it, taking great liberties with the details.

I get it. For some outlets, the more sensationalised the story, the bigger the potential boost in ratings, viewers, or readers. In other words: it's not personal; it's just business.

Now as disappointed as I was about not getting a real present that day, I still felt moved to share my story in the hopes that it might help other people to feel less alone. Which means when other journalists have requested an interview, I've most often said yes.

Some of these interviews have resulted in wonderful, heartfelt, and deeply compassionate conversations and articles. Others have been the equivalent of the great wine bottle fiasco.

Whenever I sit down with a journalist now, try as I might to calm myself, I can't help but feel anxious at first, like the rug is about to be pulled out from under me. That single experience colours my view of all other journalists. The reporter sitting in front of me might be a perfectly nice and good and decent person, but my perception has been tainted. *It's not them; it's me.* Because of my personal experiences, it's hard for me to trust them again, but I'm working on it.

We're all like that: carrying around old wounds and scars we're often not even aware of. These experiences can drive our anxiety or trigger us in different situations, in ways we might not even understand.

Other people do this too. Which is one of the biggest reasons we should never take anything personally. Every person is a walking jumble of their past experiences and interactions.

If someone is rude or mean to you, it may not be that they don't like *you, per se.* It may be that on some subconscious level, you remind them of that person who once broke their heart, was mean to them, or stole their lunch money in the third grade.

Not always, of course. Sometimes two personalities just don't gel, as much as we want them to. But either way, it doesn't mean there's something wrong with you.

Likewise, it could simply be that there's other stuff going on in their lives and hearts that we know nothing about. When people are in pain, sometimes they can't help but to smear that pain all over others. As the saying goes, hurt people hurt people.

Decades ago, when I lived in London, I so desperately longed to be in a relationship. Every time I saw a happy couple lolling in the park, or out grocery shopping together, it tore my heart in two.

On Valentine's Day each year, my single girlfriends and I went out and got smashed, sauntering around the West End and jeering like maniacs at any couple who dared to flaunt their bliss or roses in our faces.

Whenever I received a party invitation from a happy couple, I'd ignore it completely, or turn up and act like a total brat about it. These lovely people had done nothing wrong. It wasn't personal. It was that I was struggling with a deep ache within and didn't have the emotional maturity to know what to do with it, so I took it out on others. Unfortunately the old adage is true that misery loves company.

If someone isn't happy for you, perhaps they're not truly happy themselves. If someone yells at you, perhaps they just got fired, or are going through a messy divorce, or had to bury a loved one. Often they're hurting, or having a bad day, and we simply get caught in the crossfire of their emotions. Because let's face it, happy people generally don't do or say hateful things. Other people's behaviours rarely have anything to do with us at all.

Throughout all the years I drank to the point of blackout, I was often paranoid about who might be mad at me, or what people thought of me. Each time the phone rang, my heart froze in terror, worried it would be someone telling me (or my partner at the time, if they were the one to answer the phone) another shameful thing I'd said or done.

It was completely understandable in early sobriety, then, to find I had a 'hangxiety' of sorts from that time. If you've ever done foolish things when drinking, perhaps you've experienced paranoia or anxiety like this of your own.

If we dig a little deeper, we might just find our deepest insecurities hiding amongst our fears that everyone is mad at us. We can jump to conclusions or invent stories in our heads, that have nothing to do with reality and everything to do with the fact that we're struggling to come to terms with our new place in the sober, mature, or emotionally healthy world we find ourselves in.

Early in March of 2020, before the world began to slam closed its borders and order residents into lockdown, I attended a large business function in my home city. Australia hadn't yet begun recommending mask wearing, or even social distancing, so two hundred of us gathered in a large ballroom, our biggest thoughts being about our excitement to see the guest speaker.

Somewhere in amongst the breakfast fun, frivolity and networking, I contracted the virus we now know as COVID-19 which, over the following weeks, proceeded to make a complete nuisance of itself and progress into viral pneumonia. It was so early in the pandemic that it came as a complete shock, and when I texted my closest friends and family members to let them know, they were floored too.

I was sicker than I'd ever been in my life, but I was so touched and encouraged by the outpouring of love and support messages I received. That is, with one very notable exception. One of my closest friends didn't respond.

Her silence baffled me. As the days dragged on, I flip-flopped between a million different scenarios in my head. Maybe she was cranky at me for something (although I couldn't imagine what), or maybe she was really freaked out about the whole pandemic situation and didn't want to hear anything about it. Maybe she was upset that our city had suddenly plunged into lockdown and didn't feel like talking to anyone or looking at her phone, or maybe she was genuinely scared for my health and didn't know what to say.

A few weeks (and a million imaginary mind stories!) after that, she called me, stunned by the news. She'd been just about to text me when she saw my message for the very first time.

Slowly, we figured out how she could have missed it. I'd sent her my message on the night she'd visited her Mum for the last time before lockdown, and when she was there, she'd let her youngest son play games on her phone.

All that energy, time and headspace *wasted,* worried that she was mad at me, or freaked out, or shitty, or scared. Nope! She simply didn't get the message. I'd made up an infinite number of stories that had nothing to do with my friend's thoughts or actions, or even reality. The stories lived entirely in my own head.

When we remember that *everyone* does this, it makes it that much easier to realise that everyone is in their own little daze, dreaming their own dream. Their reality is shaped by their own perception, and therefore the vast majority of their thoughts, beliefs and actions have nothing to do with us at all.

Each of us is simply seeing things through the lens of our own emotions, beliefs, and past experiences. Or, to say it another way: we don't see things as they are, we see things as *we* are.

This epiphany is kind of freeing, don't you think? When we realise that the vast majority of things are not personal, we're liberated to be more of who we truly are. We can then spend less time making up stories in our own heads, and more time being compassionate towards others, as we all attempt to figure out this wild and kooky thing called life.

8. Approval Addiction

Not taking things personally is one thing, of course, especially when we actually know or have at least *met* the person. But what the fudge are we supposed to do with blatant criticism from external forces that still feels extremely personal?

We're in the tech age now, baby, and that means we've never been more exposed to the opinions of others. This can be a blessing when it comes to finding groups of people online who love the same movies as us, or are just as obsessed with baking choc chip cookies as we are. It's a blast to find and bond with our people.

But on the flip side, it can also send us spiralling into an abyss of procrastination, terrified to ever put a foot wrong in case we're criticised or judged for it.

In the years before I began helping people with sobriety, I channeled my corporate and blogging background into helping other health coaches to grow their businesses so they could help more people. In the course of that work, one of the biggest fears I saw come up time and again was the fear of being seen, and in particular, the fear of being criticised. Heck, I felt it too. Whether it's posting on social media about our latest blog post, hand-drawn sketch, or thriving petunia garden, sharing our creations can make us feel like we're back in the third grade, holding up our art project in front of the entire class.

One day soon after my first book was published, I was walking around the river with my friend, Sophie. The sun was shining, the birds were chirping, and we were chatting about how relieved and thrilled I was to have actually finished the process.

"It's such a huge milestone," Sophie said. "Have you had much feedback on it? What are people saying?"

"Well!" I said dramatically, pausing to take a deep breath. "Most of the reviews have been so beautiful. We're reaching more people than ever before, and their love letters have brought me to tears. But..." I giggled. "Some people hated it. And I mean *hated* it."

"*What!*", Sophie gasped, clutching her chest. "Oh my *God,* that's my worst nightmare! What did you *do?* How do you *cope?*"

The fact is, there's a flip side to sending your work out into the world: some people just won't like it. It's simply a numbers game. Reaching more people and playing a bigger game also means gaining more critics. It's par for the course.

You could keep yourself small, of course. That's always an option. But when you're ninety years old and you look back at your life, do you think you'll say, 'I'm so glad I never gave anyone the chance to criticise me or my work / art / parenting skills', or 'I really wish I'd switched careers / expanded my family / pursued my dream'?

Later that same year, I was invited to showcase my book on a large international website, and again I found those pesky old fears rise up. To be honest, I almost psyched myself out of accepting the opportunity altogether, worrying myself silly about what their audience is like, whether it'd be a safe space, and whether they'd like me. For days, I obsessed, imagining every possible end-of-the-world scenario.

Finally (much to Dom's relief), I realised how absurd I was being. There are no guarantees in life, only choices. Did I have the courage to follow my heart and spread my message, reaching as many people as possible? Or was I going to wimp out, play it safe, and eternally wonder about what might have been?

One of my friends, Cassie, is an incredible inspiration to me in this department. She is hands-down one of the most amazing, warm, and caring people I've ever met, and yet due to her staggering success, there are entire forums and websites dedicated to viciously tearing her down. When her community rushes to her defence, she often tells them: "It's okay. I'm not here for the haters. I'm here to shine my light as brightly as possible and encourage you to shine yours."

Pretty classy, huh? It reminds me of the beautiful Marianne Williamson quote: "Your playing small does not serve the world. There is nothing enlightened about shrinking so that other people won't feel insecure around you. We are all meant to shine, as children do… It's not just in some of us; it's in everyone. And as we let our own light shine, we unconsciously give other people permission to do the same. As we are liberated from our own fear, our presence automatically liberates others."

The truth is, it's much easier to criticise something than it is to create something. Not only is the critic viewing our work through the lens of their own perception and past experiences, but who knows: they may even be jealous that you finally started a blog when they don't have the courage to, or that you have a fun new painting hobby while they wish they could live a more creative life.

During an interview once, a podcast host asked me about the very personal details I so openly shared in my first book. We were chatting on video as well as audio at the time, when she leaned in towards the screen and asked, "So what's it like, having so many people essentially read your diary and feel like they know you?"

The truth is, it's bizarre. The very thought of it was enough to make me want to puke at first (hello, vulnerability hangover!), until I realised that each person was reading my story completely differently. Every person was viewing it through their own lens.

People often wrote things in reviews or in letters to me, like "I loved the part where you did such-and-such", even though I'd never said or written anything even remotely close to that. They'd clearly projected their own interpretation into the book because they needed that particular message for some reason.

All of this hails back to not taking anything personally, of course, but also the fact that people may criticise you no matter what. Even if you choose to play it safe and do nothing courageous in life, you can bet your bottom dollar someone will judge you for being boring, lazy or unambitious. So really, what have you got to lose? There's no reason not to follow your heart.

If you put something new out into the world and receive hurtful criticism, you might like to do what I do and immediately focus on the good reviews. I turn my attention to all the people I'm helping or bringing joy to. They're who I'm ultimately doing the work for, after all. They're the people I'm looking to connect with.

Meditation can also work wonders. Slowing down my breath and reconnecting with my deeper self and the magic of our galaxy reminds me that I'm just a tiny part of a greater whole. I'm just one speck of dust in comparison to the Universe at large. This concept helps me to put things into perspective and remember that my best laid plans (or hopes to never be judged harshly) are only half the story; the rest is not up to me.

Then I get back up, and continue to look forward,

create, and do what I feel like I'm here to do. I mean, if you think about it, there are plenty of people out there who can't stand Stephen King's books. Do you think he's losing sleep over it? *No way,* he's too busy having fun writing the next one.

Deep down, I know it's not my purpose to spend this precious life worrying about what people think of me on any given day. It's my purpose to follow my heart, and create things I feel called to share in the hopes of helping others and making this world a better place. To keep evolving, growing, and making *myself* proud.

The next time you let fear of criticism stop you from stepping onto a larger stage, ask yourself: is the criticism constructive? Is it coming from someone you admire?

Happy, successful people are much more likely to give you ways you can improve, genuinely wanting to help you to become all you can be. Emotionally unhealthy people, or those in their own kind of pain, are much more inclined to tell you all the ways you messed up, or all the things they see wrong with you or your creation. Either way, we get to choose whose opinions or feedback we allow in.

Unfortunately, the vast majority of criticism isn't constructive at all. Beyond all the personal reasons that someone may not like you or your work, often it's simply someone's opinion. Just like some people don't like ice-cream (I know, right?), or the colour blue. It's simply preference, and trying to convince them that blue ice-cream is a special kind of heaven on earth is a complete waste of time. They like what they like, and so do you.

And if all of this is true, it'd be pretty daft to let a few random comments or unsolicited feedback hold you back from pursuing your dreams and creating everything your heart desires, right?

Trust me, I get that it hurts sometimes. When you truly care about the thing you've created, it can be heartbreaking to hear people talk smack about it. It can make you want to run for the hills and never try anything ever again. The sooner you can release your need for approval, therefore, the freer you will become.

I once had the honour of interviewing Approval Addiction Specialist Amy Pearson, who shared with me a powerful tool she uses with her clients. It goes something like this:

One third of the world will always be critics. No matter what we do; no matter how hard we try, or how fabulous our shoes or jokes are, they just won't like us. One third of the world will always be neutral. They could take us or leave us. Total indifference. And one third of the world are *our* people. They totally get us, and think we're the best thing since spiced olives.

The problem is, we often spend *way* too much time trying to win over the first two camps. We might dress differently, or speak differently, in an effort to get them to like us. Carry on like this for too long, and we begin to forget who we are. Our sparkle fades. We become a shadow of our true selves.

Suddenly the third group can no longer recognise us as one of them. Heck, we barely recognise *ourselves* anymore. And so we appeal to *no-one*. We feel isolated, disconnected, and lost. Losing ourselves further at the bottom of the bottle, or in any other numbing, addictive behaviour, feels ever more seductive.

And oh boy, could I recognise this behaviour in myself. My approval fix came in many forms: appreciation, praise, compliments; but most especially in acceptance and love. When I received those things, I felt temporarily happy and safe. And yet, there was always part of me that was terrified it could all be taken away at any given moment.

I could never fully relax, because underneath that fleeting illusion of safety was the trapdoor to my deepest fears of rejection, abandonment, and criticism.

This underlying anxiety was a constant presence. It was always there, in my desperate need to be liked by everyone; the way other people had so much control over my feelings; and that every piece of criticism - or even the smallest slight - always felt highly personal and completely devastating.

Back in 2011 when I first started a little recipe blog, I opened myself up to worldwide criticism for the first time. With the comments fields open on my blog posts, anyone with a laptop could tell me exactly what they thought of me or my 'stupid recipes' - and many did! A lot of people loved my kitchen creations, but some thought they were the worst thing they'd ever had the misfortune of putting into their mouths. Or that my cheery disposition was incredibly annoying. Or that I was a complete idiot and my measurements or ingredients were all off.

But guess what? I didn't die. I thought I would at the time, mind you. I thought not being liked was the worst thing in the entire world. I cried each time I received a mean comment, and stewed on it for days. But with each one, I began to see that it was impossible to please every single person in the world. And that that was okay.

Naturally, I would have preferred that they gave me helpful suggestions rather than go all 'keyboard warrior' on me, but that was their choice. Mine was in how I chose to pick myself back up and move on.

As children, we often learn that we win praise and love when we're 'good'. As a result, some of us *(hello!)* can find it difficult to distinguish who we are from what we do: between our value as a person, and our behaviour (or our art!). When our actions or creations are criticised, we can therefore find ourselves becoming overly defensive or distraught, as though our entire worth as a human being has been invalidated and devalued.

The emotional baggage of our childhood can find us finely tuned to the slightest hint of disapproval from others, and make us respond to criticism with intense anxiety. In people-pleasing habits formed over a lifetime, whereby we're quick to yield control to others, we'll do nearly anything to reduce the painful fear of abandonment triggered by criticism, disapproval, or even the whiff of a clue that we're not liked.

One of the biggest lessons in life and growth I've ever had to endure is the willingness to let this go. Not everyone can understand or approve of us, and even if they could, it's not their job. It's ours. What we think of ourselves is infinitely more powerful than anything anyone else could ever think of us.

What if we stopped tap-dancing for approval from those who will never be ready, willing or able to give it, and instead focused on the one-third? What if we focused all our love and energy into going deeper into our connection with the people who are already on our team, or our wavelength? Wouldn't that be liberating?

Look for that one-third. They're those special souls who truly *see* you; who are endlessly support- ive, encouraging and kind. The people you feel safe to completely yourself around. They're out there, and they're looking for you too. Focus on them, and love them, and watch what happens.

When we spend more time with these people, we feel good about ourselves. We remember who we are. We give more approval to ourselves, so we stop seeking it from others. And then, we feel truly free.

9. Boundaries Will Set You Free

Many years ago, I worked in an office that had really great morale. I was on a fun team and was friends with most of my colleagues, including Paul, the guy who sat next to me. We often joked around in the office, went to pubs together after work, and made each other laugh as we waited for meetings to start, or at office functions.

Everything was fine and dandy until one day, a new guy was brought in to sit next to Paul. His name was Gavin, and he was a few years older than us. He wore faded striped shirts that were ten years past their prime, and a permanent smirk.

Technically, Gavin and Paul were ever so slightly

senior in role to the rest of our team of ten, but we'd never felt the difference from Paul before. Our desks were all grouped together in our large, open plan office, and we'd always felt like a well oiled machine, working together. We thought once Gavin warmed up he'd fit in well too, like the rest of us.

We thought wrong.

As the weeks became months, Gavin and Paul became closer. Gavin invited Paul along to management meetings and golf days, and they were often found sniggering and scoffing together over something on Gavin's computer screen.

Slowly, Paul started acting more like Gavin, smirking and speaking down to the rest of our team. He'd always been more than happy to show us how to complete a new task, or jump in to help us whenever the workload was too much for us to get through alone. But now, he started barking orders, rolling his eyes, and sighing at us like we were wayward children he was forced to supervise.

It bugged me that he was being so rude, but because it started slowly, it seemed easier to let it go at first. Me being the people-pleaser I was, I didn't say anything, instead hoping it would all magically resolve itself.

Of course it didn't. In fact, the longer I stayed quiet, the worse it became. Until one fateful afternoon.

"Re-*be*-cca," Paul said slowly, in a tone so patronising, my heart sank. "Do you know how to put together one of these reports?"

He glanced sideways at Gavin and they both

smirked.

My first thought was: *what the hell?* I wasn't his secretary, for crying out loud! He'd always collated his own damn reports; what made this one so special? I was more than happy to pitch in to help if he asked nicely, but not simply so he could feel superior and show off to his sidekick.

"Of course," I said through clenched teeth, turning back to my computer and hoping and praying that was the end of it.

No such luck.

"Well then, could you do *this one*, please?" Paul said haughtily, waving the report papers above me like an older brother attempting to aggravate a sibling.

Without warning, a white hot fury filled my body. In any conflict, there's always a final straw - a reckoning - and it seemed this moment was destined to be it.

"Yessss!" I hissed, snatching the papers from his hands.

All those times he'd been condescending and I hadn't said anything - all those times I'd let him get away with it - simmered dangerously through my veins. As I stood up from my desk, I tried to control myself, but it was no use. My body and voice shook with resentment and rage as I finally roared, "BUT DON'T SPEAK TO ME LIKE I'M AN IDIOT!"

Instantly, dozens of heads popped up over computer screens, their mouths gaping at the commotion as I turned and stormed off to the printer room.

There I stood, attempting to calm myself down

and willing myself not to cry, when Sam, a friend from another team, came to find me.

"Are you alright?" He said, his eyes like saucers. "We could hear you from around the corner!"

I'd never lost my temper with anyone at work before, so I can only imagine hearing me screaming across the office came as a bit of a shock.

"Ugh!" I ranted. "They can just be such assholes when they're together! I'm so sick of it!"

"I know," he said, kindness and compassion written all over his face. "But just try to keep it together, hey? You're leaving soon."

Indeed I was. I'd already handed in my resignation and had only a couple of weeks remaining in my notice period before I moved back to my home city.

I sighed and nodded, and managed a small smile. "You're right. Thanks."

As Sam left me to go back to his desk, I felt much better. And more than that, I realised my over-reaction was, in large part, self-induced. I hadn't made it clear to Paul that his behaviour or comments were making me uncomfortable (or downright furious). For all I knew, he might have thought I'd found it funny. I was ninety percent sure that their jabs were for their own amusement rather than the amusement of others, but - call me an optimist - there was always that ten percent chance, right?

Taking a deep breath, I headed back to my desk. As I sat down, for some reason the whole messy situation struck me as kind of funny. I was embarrassed about my behaviour, and I figured Paul was probably also embarrassed about his. We were once great friends, after all. It was time to put all this behind us.

I thought about leaning over to apologise but, childish as I was back then, I changed my mind. *Let him stew on it for a day. We can figure it out tomorrow.*

The funny thing about tomorrow is that it never comes.

We didn't speak the following day, or the day after that. I figured we'd for sure make up before I left work for good, but every time I tried to catch his eye and smile, or find him alone so I could say sorry, he was having none of it.

Looking back now, I realise I could have insisted on pulling him aside, and explained what had happened from my perspective; the chain of events that had triggered me to react so strongly. I could have apologised for waiting until my nerves were so frazzled that I'd called him out on it like a sociopath in front of the entire office floor.

He might have then apologised for acting like a massive turd-burger, or told me something that made his behaviour make more sense. Or perhaps he was even completely unaware that his behaviour had changed and that our whole team felt this way.

We'll never know for sure, because while I kept in contact with most of my other friends from that team, Paul and I never spoke again.

In a misguided but well-meaning attempt to spare Paul's feelings and preserve our friendship (as well as save myself the embarrassment of making it all into a 'big thing'), I'd chosen to stay quiet. If I'd asked him not to speak to me like that the first time, the whole situation probably wouldn't have escalated like it did. Instead, I repeatedly failed to ask him politely to stop, until I finally reached my tipping point and unleashed unholy hell onto him.

In retrospect, I would have saved all this drama, as well as potentially our friendship, by clearly establishing my boundaries as soon as they'd been violated.

Sadly, this was nothing new to me. As a people-pleaser, I waited too long to say no to virtually everyone. I was emotionally black and blue from the constant invasion of my personal boundaries. My desperate attempt to be endlessly amicable and compliant meant that rather than situations being calmly and easily resolved, they were allowed to fester until the stench grew so bad that I totally lost it and blew up, often permanently damaging the relationship by saying something I could never take back.

Boundaries might sound like some kind of great big fence designed to keep other people out, but they can actually help protect and strengthen relationships. Boundaries are honest; they get everything out onto the table.

I must admit, I didn't get it at first. When I was drinking, all the lines in my life were incredibly blurred, and even if I'd been capable of understanding them, I lacked the self esteem required to actually communicate and uphold them. I thought boundaries meant telling people how they should behave around me, which felt so odd and diva-like. It took me a long time to understand that boundaries are about *my* self-care, rather than trying to get others to act in a particular way.

Creating boundaries is like drawing a large circle around myself that ensures I feel safe to be completely me. Healthy boundaries show other people that this person is loved and cared for, and that if you choose to disrespect her, you will not be allowed to come any closer.

That is, our love shows people that we want them in our lives; our boundaries show them *how* we want them as part of our lives.

This is also a great reminder that we teach other people how to treat us. If we need something, we should ask for it. People are not mind readers, as much as we hope or think they should be. We might have to actually communicate and, you know, use our words rather than telepathy.

Dom has always been an incredible teacher to me in this area, never afraid to speak up or tell others how he wants to be treated. When we first moved in together, I almost had a stroke when I overheard him telling a relative on the phone, "Now, make sure you call us before you visit. Don't just rock up."

"Oh my God," I spluttered as he hung up the phone. "I can't believe you said that!" Half of me was so impressed I could barely stand it; the other half was completely mortified.

We're both introverts by nature, and generally not fans of the pop-in visit, preferring to have plenty of notice in which to prepare ourselves. But holy guacamole, was it really okay to *tell* people to call first? There's no way in a million *years* I would have had the gall to request that of anyone.

What if they thought I was rude? What if they decided I was too difficult and not only never visited, but told everyone else how painful I was, and no-one ever visited me again?

Ohhh, it was a scary, scary place in my people-pleasing mind.

"Huh?" Dom looked over at me, genuinely baffled. "Said what?"

"The 'call first' thing!" I spluttered some more.

"Why? Do you want people to just rock up?"

"Well, no." I replied.

"So tell them that," he shrugged.

Well, sure, it all sounded so sane and logical when he said it like that. I mean, it was all so mature and grown-up: actually *communicating* your preferences rather than, say, diving under the couch whenever the doorbell rang unexpectedly.

It was at about this point that I realised I might have to investigate the fears underlying my inability or unwillingness to be honest about what I truly wanted.

Setting healthy boundaries is a topic that continues to fascinate me, precisely because there was a time when I had no idea what they were or how to implement them. I was always so scared to say no to anyone

who asked for anything. I was terrified of confrontation or making waves; afraid people wouldn't like me if
I was honest; too insecure to clearly state that I wasn't
able or willing to give them what they'd asked of me.

And it was because of this people-pleasing that
I often found myself boiling over with resentment
as people continued to overstep their mark and take
advantage of me (often without them even being aware
of it!).

Boundaries will set you free. They set the basic
guidelines of how you want to be treated. Of course,
establishing boundaries requires courage in speaking up, telling the truth, and asking for what you
need. It involves overcoming potentially *decades* of
people-pleasing tendencies. For me, it felt like finally
growing a backbone.

The truth of the matter is that when you've had
zero boundaries for a very long time, suddenly standing up for yourself can create ripples throughout your
relationships. Some people won't like your new boundaries. They may feel offended or cheated by the fact
that you're now standing up for yourself or having the
gall to finally tell them that their toxic or inconvenient
behaviour is unacceptable.

Some people might push your buttons just to test
your resolve, or get emotional when you stand up for
yourself. That's entirely their choice, but here's what
you need to remember: it doesn't have anything to do
with you. Their reactions are not your responsibility.
You don't owe anyone an apology for taking care of

yourself.

Most people who love you will respect your boundaries because they want you to be happy and healthy. And those who don't, may have to remain outside your inner circle until they do.

The key to navigating this new level in our relationships is to approach it all with honesty, compassion, and clear communication. Begin to notice the things that make you feel uncomfortable, and speak up as quickly as possible (and well before you find yourself shouting your head off across an entire office floor).

When we've shoved down our true thoughts and emotions for a long time, speaking up takes an incredible act of faith and courage. It requires us to be vulnerable and risk rejection or ridicule.

But you know what? It's also incredibly empowering, because as we learn to uphold boundaries, we become more honest about what's really going on for us, and in communicating what we need. We grow in self-worth.

And what awaits us on the other side of our fear is a deeper feeling of connection; of authenticity; of finally belonging to ourselves.

10. Prioritise Saying No

Back in the early 2000's, I had one of those tiny flip phones. Less than the size of my palm and a deep plum colour, it had white flowers etched into the front, and a tiny sparkly charm dangling from the antenna. One morning I was turning this glorious little device over in my palm, admiring it from every angle as I often loved to do, when it started to ring.

It was an old friend calling out of the blue. We hadn't spoken in months and I was delighted to hear from her. She lived overseas so I was even more surprised when she said, "Hey Bex, could I ask a favour? Could I come stay with you for a few days?"

In retrospect, the phrasing of that sentence should have been my first clue. The strange sensation in my gut should have been the other warning. But we hadn't seen each other for years, and I was thrilled with the idea.

Okay, so the date she was flying in was right smack bang in the middle of a big project at work, but I couldn't come out and actually *tell* her that. Besides, I figured if I somehow managed to hustle my bustle and work ludicrous hours, maybe, just maybe, I'd be able to take off the entire five days of her visit.

For the next few weeks I worked eleven hours a day, weekends included, determined to clear my calendar so I could have a grand adventure with her. I was highly motivated, I was a woman on a mission, and nothing was going to stop me!

By the time I picked her up from the airport, I was a wild mix of exhaustion and elation. *I'd done it!* It was an incredibly inconvenient time to take off work, and I'd very nearly killed myself in the process, but *by jove*, we were going to have so much fun!

Only, it appeared I'd completely missed the memo. On the drive home, my friend promptly and cheerfully informed me that her week was almost entirely full of catch-ups with other people. My time wouldn't be required at all.

To say I was shocked, confused and devastated is an understatement. As this little info nugget sank in and my fingers gripped the steering wheel, it dawned on me that she'd simply wanted somewhere to stay, not someone to hang out with beyond our initial greeting lunch.

Naturally, since my fear of confrontation was

greater than my desire for honest communication, I didn't attempt to talk to her about this. Instead, I simply gave her my spare key and allowed her to go on her merry way, later sobbing myself to sleep.

Oh boy, there's so much to unpack about this. There was my lack of foresight or confidence to directly ask her about her plans in the first place. There was my lack of communication about what a difficult time it was for me at work and what I'd have to do in order to clear my calendar for her. There was my expectation that when she asked to come stay, it was so we could spend the week together. And finally, and most spectacularly, there was my fear of confrontation manifesting in my inability to speak honestly with her about my crushing disappointment.

If there's one phrase that has always been guaranteed to make me squeamish, it's: "Can you do me a favour?"

Oh, those triggering little words. For years I didn't understand why they filled me with utter dreaded. I hated them with a passion and thought it so unbelievably rude that someone would demand to hijack my time like that, without even having the decency or manners to tell me what the favour was before trapping me. *I mean, what kind of person has the audacity to just come out and SAY that kind of thing to another?*

As it turns out, a confident and well-adjusted one.

It took me a long time to understand that it wasn't the request itself that was so horrifying to me - it was simply the fact that I didn't know how to say no.

That is, it wasn't them; it was *me*.

Saying no would lead me down a rabbit hole of unwanted emotions, ranging from guilt to shame to feeling like a terrible person. Not to mention opening myself up to the risk of experiencing conflict, rejection, abandonment, disapproval, or anger.

As a people-pleaser, I wanted everyone around me to be happy and would do pretty much whatever was asked of me to keep it that way. Although I wasn't yet aware of it, underneath those people-pleasing tendencies was a yearning for outside validation. My security and self-confidence were based on winning the approval of others. I worried about how others would react if I didn't comply. I didn't want to be seen as self-ish, uncaring or lazy in their eyes, and I was scared I'd be disliked or excluded if I was honest with them.

So I said yes. Always. Regardless of whether I didn't want to do the favour, didn't have the time, or didn't particularly like the person who was asking. I said yes because deep down I believed it was the safer route.

Little did I realise that saying yes to things I really didn't want to do *also* led me down a rabbit hole; only this one resulted in me becoming a very frustrated and resentful little bunny. Often, even mere seconds after I'd agreed to the request, I'd find myself flooded with annoyance at the person who had so effectively manip-ulated my niceness and my inability to say no.

To add insult to injury, I'd immediately feel guilty and ashamed for harbouring such feelings. Then I'd feel bad about myself, further chipping away at my flaky self-esteem.

Of course, it's possible that some colleagues and fair-weather friends actively sought me out because they knew I was a pushover and would never say no. But, unbeknownst to me then, the truth was, I always held the power.

My strategy, therefore, became to completely avoid people who slung their requests around willy nilly, believing that by hiding, I could protect myself from feeling any of those negative emotions. In reality, by doing this, I was robbing myself of the chance to practice saying no. By avoiding them, I was reinforcing my fear of conflict and confrontation, and further stunting my growth. I was also isolating myself, hiding from people who I potentially could have experienced a deeper level of connection or relationship with. I was sacrificing my chance at true intimacy, honesty, and authenticity with others.

This dysfunctional chain of thought also robbed me of my ability to ask anyone *else* for help. After all, if I hated people asking it of *me*, I'd never want to put anyone else through that. So I simply never asked for help. Ever. And yet, often I secretly longed for someone to swoop in and rescue me. Doing everything myself was exhausting.

Once again I was operating under a flawed strategy that led to me feeling resentful and isolated, wondering why on earth no-one was offering to help me.

Of course, there's a huge difference between people-pleasing and simply doing nice things for others. Picking up an extra choc chip muffin for your work friend, or collecting your friend's border collie from the dog wash because her car broke down are examples of being a kind and considerate human.

People-pleasing, on the other hand, is when our welfare and happiness are sacrificed for the sake of somebody else's. It feels different due to the energy behind it. That is, we *want* to help, versus we feel obligated or pressured to help, but really don't want to.

There was also another, deeper, darker truth I didn't understand at the time: when it all came down to brass tacks, by saying yes when I didn't want to, I was effectively attempting to manipulate people into liking me. I was subconsciously 'social engineering' the situation to avoid what I was most afraid of: confrontation or rejection. I thought being agreeable made me a good person, but what if it just made me a manipulative one?

The problem was, I'd never gotten clear on my priorities before, and it showed.

When I first started working for myself, I was enthusiastic and eager to please, and said yes to anything and everything that even hinted at being an exciting opportunity. As our business grew and I became known as the 'yes' girl, I was gradually inundated with requests. Even though my own workload had increased ten-fold, still I said yes.

Would I like to write an unpaid, three thousand word feature article for an up-and-coming website that needs to be in by this Friday? *I'd love to!*

Would I like to be part of an upcoming summit

that requires tens of hours of work with no pay or any kind of guarantee of exposure? *I'd be honoured!*

Would I like to test and review someone's recipe, even though the dish sounds godawful? *You betcha!*

If I was asked, I said yes. Even if it meant working myself silly. I mean, it'd be rude to say no, wouldn't it? What if I turned it down and never received another opportunity?

It doesn't take a genius to figure out that this kind of pressure and work load leads straight to burn-out. In desperation, I started reading books by other creatives and entrepreneurs, and took note when they said that in order to focus on the work that matters most to them, they say no to ninety-nine percent of the requests they receive.

Whether in business or in life, we all have only twenty four hours in a day. We all have just one life in which to live out every goal, dream or experience we desire. In other words, my time is precious, and so is yours. Once we give it away, we can't ever get it back.

I'd never stopped to consider what my highest priorities were or made any kind of conscious choice about what I actually wanted to spend my time on. When I sat down to think about this, I realised my top priorities are deep connection with close friends and family, creative work, and taking care of my health.

Yours might have to do with your life's work, your finances, mental health, self improvement, or relationships. What do you care about? What matters most to you? Not what's most important to your parents or your friends; what are *you* most passionate about?

Since you're human, it's likely that at least one of your priorities will have something to do with the people in your life. Who are you closest to? Who would you do anything for? Whose doorstep could you show up on in the middle of the night and be welcomed in, and vice versa?

Those are the people to focus on; the relationships worth making time for. Casual acquaintances, colleagues from a job you left fifteen years ago, and friends-of-friends - as nice as they may be - don't need to merit top priority (except, of course, in unusual or emergency situations where people may really need our one-off help).

Another way to get clear on your top priorities is to think about your big life goals and dreams. Where do you want to be three years from now? What do you want to have experienced in that time? How about in ten years? Or twenty? Write out your most audacious dream in big, juicy detail. This vision may shift and change with time of course, but even just thinking about it will give you clarity around what matters most to you and what lights you up.

Once you're clear on these priorities, people, and goals, it becomes so much easier to say no to (or prioritise) other things and people that attempt to chew up your time. Behind every 'no' is a 'yes': to more time with your inner circle of loved ones, for self-care, for pursuing a dream or taking a class or volunteering for a cause that you really believe in.

Practice saying no as often as you can, even if you don't always know what to say.

When I was in my twenties and working in London, a guy from work sent me an email asking me out to lunch. He worked on a different floor, in a completely different department, and I was single and wanting a boyfriend, so I thought: *why not?*

We went to a bank-that-had-been-transformed-in-to-a-bar around the corner from our office and ordered some food, and at first he seemed nice and normal enough. But as the conversation began to flow, every few minutes or so he made a rude, obnoxious, or passive-aggressive dig at me.

When I ordered a drink, he pulled a face and asked if I was "one of those massive boozers" (alright, so perhaps I was at that point, but I sure as hell wasn't ready to be called out on it on a first date!).

When I commented on the stunning Art Deco mirror border that ran around the tops of the walls, he asked if I was "really vain or something?"

He complimented my top and then immediately followed it up with a smirk and "shop at H&M often, do you?"

In short, it was the worst date I'd ever been on. I scoffed half my meal down as quickly as possible and practically sprinted back to the office. *Why had he even bothered to ask me out if he was going to spend the entire time insulting me?*

When I reached the safety of my desk, I chalked the whole thing up to experience and thanked the ever-loving stars that he worked far, far away from me and we'd never have to see each other again.

Or so I thought.

Less than thirty minutes later, as I was still trying to get over my irritation by busying myself in work, a new email popped into my inbox.

It was him.

Oh, what now? I thought, inhaling sharply as I clicked on it.

But instead of the crappy note I'd expected, he raved about what a great time he'd had, and asked if I'd like to "go out to dinner sometime?"

I was astounded. *Was he even on the same date?!* I would have rather spent ten years alone in the wilderness than spend more time with him.

After my initial shock, came resentment. *Why was it now MY problem to have to find a way to tell him that?*

Wanting to run as far away from my computer and his message as possible, I bolted to the other end of my department's floor. There were filing cabinets up there: not my favourite task, by any means, but if it meant I could hide within them for the rest of my working career, I could definitely get used to doing filing full-time, sure I could.

I was just getting stuck into the second tray of folders and attempting to push the whole messy thing out of my mind when one of my colleagues walked by. One of the only other women in my department, Olivia was smart, sophisticated, and in her thirties. She'd know what to do.

In a flash of courage and inspiration, I called out to her. "Hey, Olivia?"

"Mm-hmm?" She turned warily back towards me, looking at the folder in my hand, clearly not wanting to be invited into my filing expedition.

Before I could chicken out, I blurted out the whole sorry tale. "So I just went on a lunch date with a guy and it was terrible and I thought he hated it as much as I did but now he's sent me a message asking me on a dinner date but I really don't want to go but I don't know what to say."

"Say no," she shrugged, and turned as though she was about to walk away.

I'm not sure if it was the desperate and sorry look on my face that made her pause, or her genuine fear that I might actually start crying in the office, but slowly she turned back to stare at me.

Sighing at my stupidity, she finally said, "Okay, so say something like: it was nice to see you today. I don't think we have enough in common to continue dating, but thank you anyway and I wish you well."

"Thank you!" I gushed, giddy with relief as she spun on her heels and sauntered away.

Taking a deep breath, I headed back to my desk and did exactly that. Even though it felt weird and awful saying no, there was also a huge part of it that felt really good. It felt mature and honest and respectful, to both of us (well, except for the part where I'd had to ask my colleague what to say, of course. *Ahem*.).

Two minutes later, another message popped into

my inbox. It was from him. Apparently he hadn't found my email mature or honest or respectful at all. He was clearly angry and his response was just as rude as his behaviour at lunch. But guess what? That only made me even more proud of myself for saying no, and eternally grateful that I'd saved myself from having to spend any more minutes of my life hanging out with him.

If you're not sure how to say no, write down a few scripts and try them out. Ask friends or colleagues what they'd say if they were in that situation. Remember that the person asking may genuinely want to spend time with you, or desire your help with something, so be as kind as possible. Think about the other person and how you'd like the 'no' delivered if you were on the receiving end.

Above all, don't run from the chance to practice (trust me, nothing exciting ever happens in the filing room). Say no in an honest and loving way so you come to understand there is nothing to fear when you do. The more you practice, the less terrifying it will become.

Saying 'no' when you mean it, will in no way diminish your value or worth in the eyes of your loved ones. In fact, as they witness you being honest and respectful of your own time, it might even enhance it.

Remember when you were a kid and you had to go to all those events you hated? For me, it was certain parties, BBQs, and sports carnivals. Oh, how this little bookworm dreaded swimming carnivals.

Well, guess what? *You're* in charge of your life now!

Saying no to the things that don't light you up, opens up time, energy, and heart space to say yes to more of the things that do.

You can still be a nice person with good intentions and say no. You can leave white space in your schedule, just because it's great for your mental health. You can decide that anything that doesn't fill you with 'HELL YES!' excitement from the tips of your toes, is a no.

You can create a life that you don't want to escape from.

11. The Danger of Not Speaking Up

When I first discovered that clear communication and conflict resolution were not inbuilt gifts for a chosen few, but actually *skills* that I could learn, it totally knocked my socks off.

For years I'd watched reality television shows, completely captivated by the cast members' seemingly magical ability to always know what to say in every situation. Whether someone was holding them accountable for their actions or confronting them about something they hadn't even done, they were totally nonplussed and seemed to have no qualms talking about the issue until it was resolved.

When someone uttered those words guaranteed to

strike an icicle of fear into my heart, "We need to talk," they didn't run off to hide in the bathroom or slip out the back door like I would. They genuinely seemed to want to clear the air and find their way to a resolution. Even their ability and willingness to express their deepest inner thoughts and emotions to each other floored me.

Is there some kind of school for that?! I wondered, utterly fascinated. *It must be an American thing, surely. They must be taught how to express their emotions in school or something.*

Then I watched similar British shows and gaped in wonder as the savvy twenty-something cast members did exactly the same thing.

Okay then, I reasoned. It must come with a certain kind of innate confidence, and either you have it or you don't.

It never occurred to me that it was a skill - like rollerskating or riding a bike - something you could actually learn (at any age) and get better at. It never crossed my mind that it was all part of developing emotional maturity and defining myself, rather than waiting for others to define me.

When I was thirty-two, my then-husband and I moved into our newly built home. It was a simple house, but it was new and it was ours and we loved it.

We'd chosen carpeting for the bedrooms, while the kitchen, dining, and living area were decked out with beautiful bamboo floorboards.

Well. It didn't take long for us to realise that our

newly installed bamboo floors didn't care for stiletto heels one little bit. The few steps I'd taken in mine had resulted in deep, ugly pockmarks across the floors.

A couple of weeks after we moved in, a bunch of my friends came over to celebrate with us, for a mini housewarming event of sorts. Knowing what we knew about the floors, before they arrived, my husband begged me to ask them to take their shoes off at the front door.

Now, these weren't scary strangers, mind you; they were some of my closest friends. I loved my friends and I loved those floors. I really didn't want any more ugly, permanent dents in them. And still, I couldn't bring myself to ask.

As they arrived and I hugged and ushered them in, closing the door behind them, I tried not to listen (or watch) as their stiletto heels click-clacked down the corridor. I knew I was betraying my husband and myself, and this home we'd dreamed of for so long, but still, I did nothing.

As is so often the case at house parties, we all formed a casual circle around the kitchen bench and started drinking, which should have given me more bravado to speak up. And *still*, I didn't want to, for fear that they'd think I was being a pain, or a fusspot, or overly precious about our new house.

And really, so what if they did think that? We would have laughed it off eventually. If they were true friends, they would have still loved me, and the floors would have remained undamaged. Instead, those poor innocent bamboo planks wore the permanent scars of my inability to speak up.

I did this kind of thing all the time; too scared to tell my loved ones what I wanted or how I felt, for fear of abandonment or rejection; worried they'd think I was too high maintenance or too precious or too *something*, and no longer want anything to do with me.

I traded my compliance for their affection and thought I was getting a good deal. But the problem with never speaking up is that people find it hard to truly connect with and trust you. You risk coming across as a one dimensional person for whom nothing's a problem, rather than a real human being with many interesting facets.

And it wasn't just my loved ones I did this with.

Once, in an annual performance review at work, my boss struggled to break it to me that for the first time in my history with that company, I'd received a mediocre score. I was flabbergasted. I didn't get it. Nothing had changed. I was always on time and efficient and pleasant and agreeable, just as I'd been every year before that. *Why didn't everyone like me?*

"Basically," my boss said, sighing as he looked up from the piece of paper in his hands, and leaned back into his chair. "Everyone agreed that you're very user-friendly. But we were hard-pressed to come up with something that really stood out about you."

Now, his unfortunate and rather bizarre choice of words aside, I guess I could see his point. I rarely spoke up in meetings because I was scared of getting something wrong and making a fool of myself. I sidestepped conflict and was way too quick to bend to the will of the more outspoken or gruff, even if they were in the wrong.

For years I completely shut down in the face of overly loud, opinionated, or aggressive people. I gave them the power to steamroll right over me and leave me feeling emotionally manipulated and resentful. I lacked the will or skills to defend myself, preferring to simply run away and steer clear of that person as much as possible in future.

I did all of this because I was scared of conflict; because deep down, I thought if I avoided conflict, I'd avoid what I was really scared of, which was rejection, scorn and abandonment.

Unfortunately, my strategy was defective. Turns out being pleasant and agreeable won't necessarily get you what you really want; like, say, a salary increase, a promotion, or the respect of your peers. Instead, you may come across as completely passive or forgettable. Which is fine if that's what you're trying to achieve; it's an effective way to fly under the radar. But if you're killing yourself trying to please other people and be liked by everyone in order to be more accepted, you might be barking up entirely the wrong tree.

This strategy of not speaking up can also cause a ton of confusion, hurt, and damage in our closest relationships. I wasn't even aware that I was doing this in romantic relationships until I stopped drinking. Slowly, as the boozy fog began to lift, I became conscious of how I behaved if Dom ever said or did something to upset me.

My typical mode of operation in those kinds of situations had always been to withhold affection; to simply shut down and become unavailable emotionally and physically. My instinct was to protect myself, so the walls went up while the pain burned itself into my chest. Meanwhile, Dom often had zero idea there was even anything the matter.

One day I was alone in our bedroom attempting to fight back tears after he'd said something (ultimately inconsequential) that had upset me. Deep down I knew it was only something silly, and yet I also knew my rights as a woman and a wife, and by golly, my right was to *get upset!* Yes, I was a grown woman sitting in her room sulking, but I was damn well going to stay in there until he came and apologised!

Suddenly a cheerful whistle came echoing down the hallway and bouncing into the room, launching an assault on my senses.

Whistling. *WHISTLING! This, from the man who had just said something that had wounded me so deeply I could barely breathe!*

A white hot fury boiled in my blood, and I flew down the hallway to the living room to confront him.

"Why are you *whistling?!*" I choked and yelled and sobbed. "I'm *mad* at you! We're *arguing!*"

Confusion, and possibly even a hint of amusement crossed Dom's face. "Huh?", he said. "We *are?*"

Confused and frustrated, I thought about stamping my foot for emphasis, but instead burst into tears.

The look all over Dom's face read, *what the hell just happened?*

As I wiped away the tears, between my remaining sobs, I started to laugh. There I was - experiencing so much emotional pain in the other room because of something he'd said - and he'd had absolutely no idea.

Clearly, I had a lot of work to do when it came to learning how to speak up, tell the truth, and ask for what I need. For eons, I'd hidden what I really felt in order to avoid rocking the boat. If something was bothering me, I ran from it, hoping it would all just go away. I had no idea how to communicate like a grown up.

And if I had a hard time confronting other people when they'd hurt me, *good grief,* did I have an even harder time being confronted about the things *I'd* done.

Years ago, I headed away with a large group of friends to celebrate our friend Vicki's birthday. I was so excited about this trip. Vicki had booked two large beach houses and I imagined us all hanging out and having silly fun all weekend. I certainly didn't imagine there'd be any conflict, or that - horror of horrors - I would be at the centre of it.

But somewhere in the amongst the festivities of the final night, I took offence to something her brother said, and swore at him. To our dismay, the birthday girl burst into tears and stormed out, wailing, *"Why can't we all just get along?!"*

I was incredibly drunk and I felt awful, of course, but I wasn't brave enough to run after her.

The next morning I woke before dawn with that special kind of anxiety reserved for hangover-fuelled regrets. Even before my eyes flew open, my stomach squirmed. *Surely it hadn't really happened? Surely I'd dreamt the whole horrid thing?*

As sunlight began to peek through my window, my bedroom door squeaked open.

"Hey," my friend Mel said softly. "Are you okay?"

Not trusting myself to say a word, I nodded tearfully. Immediately Mel jumped into the bed and wrapped herself around me in a giant spoon hug. Her kindness felt like much more than I deserved. Silently I began sobbing.

"Awww," she murmured, hugging me closer. "I know. Life can be so hard sometimes."

I'd never had a friend show me love and compassion like that before, and her kind gesture made me sob even harder. I wanted to thank her; to tell her how much she meant to me, but I lacked the communication skills to even speak up about the *good* things.

I was so deeply humiliated and sick with remorse. I was sure I'd single-handedly ruined my friend's birthday and the entire trip. I dreaded having to go out and face everyone at breakfast.

When I finally pulled myself together enough to venture out to the living room, I hung my head in shame and avoided all eye contact. Vicki was happily chatting away to everyone else and seemed to have recovered from her outburst from the night before. I was fairly sure she wouldn't yell at me, and yet I still couldn't bring myself to simply pull her aside and say sorry. *Perhaps if I tried hard enough, I could just sweep the elephant under the rug like it had never existed?*

Vicki and I were never as close after that, and was it really any wonder? My inability to take full responsibility for my actions and choke out an apology meant there was always an element of mistrust between us.

Not speaking up damages relationships. I thought ignoring conflict meant we could all just pretend it had never happened, but of course it didn't. That's not friendship; it's delusion.

It made total sense that for so many years I was terrified any time anyone 'wanted to talk' or had 'a bone to pick' with me. Experiencing regular blackouts from drinking meant I never knew when I might have upset someone or what other nonsense 'Drunk Me' might have gotten up to. I could never decide which was worse: the not-knowing, or actually being made aware of the hurtful things I'd said and done. I lived in constant fear of being outed for being a terrible or useless human being.

Now that I'm sober and devoted to doing the deep work of healing, I *want* to know if or when I do these things. As we become more emotionally healthy, we crave authenticity. I want my loved ones to tell me if I've messed up so I can become better, but also so that we get to know even more about each other, and our relationship grows ever deeper and stronger.

The hard truth is, we need conflict. If executed correctly, it strengthens our bonds with loved ones. It enables us to clear the air and to see things through each other's eyes. It allows us to define our own boundaries and to reach a new level of respect, understanding, and intimacy.

I'm not saying it's easy - learning these skills takes time, practice, and patience - but it's infinitely worthwhile, because if you're feeling angry with someone rather than resolving the issue, who is it going to do more harm to? If you're constantly hiding, or feeling anguish over people being mad at you, how will you ever feel free?

We *can* get better at this. If your relationships are important to you, they deserve your honesty. They deserve open communication.

They deserve the real you.

12. Loving Conflict

When I was eighteen, my Mum got engaged to the kind, loving man I've had the honour of calling my Step-Dad ever since. Everyone in the family was excited about the wedding, and my grandmother, being a talented seamstress, was tasked with making brides-maid dresses that suited both my sister and I.

There was just one problem. I was a moody teen-ager and had invited my new boyfriend to the event. I didn't want a dress that suited everyone; I wanted a dress that made me look amazing so he'd fall in love with me.

One day I went to my Nan's house for a fitting. I let myself in via the back patio door and found her already in her sewing room.

"Hi, love," she said, clearing away a pile of dress

patterns so I could sit down. "Your Mum said you're not happy with your dress."

Nan was never one to beat around the bush. Hormones and indignation ricocheted throughout my body. I shrugged and attempted to nod.

"You don't need to add to her stress though," Nan said in a kind tone, as she began measuring my neck for a mid-90's ribbon style choker. "She told me to 'just tighten this around her throat until she stops talking'." Nan chuckled at their shared joke.

I blushed and pulled a face, ashamed and embarrassed that they'd talked about me.

"C'mon, now," Nan said, threading cotton onto her sewing machine. "You're happy for her and her big day, aren't you?"

Instantly, my heart began to melt. Of course I was. I'd gotten so caught up in my own fears and anxieties, I'd completely lost sight of the bigger picture. With one little loving sentence, the conflict evaporated. Nan had managed to shift my entire perspective back to what really mattered: love and being there for each other. Instead of snapping at me for behaving like a brat (which I absolutely was) and potentially making the conflict worse, she led with love. Her simple, gentle questions dissolved the drama, and brought everyone closer together.

My grandmother was such a great teacher to me in this area. With kindness and generosity of spirit, using a simple sentence or tone, she encouraged me to be a better human. Her loving and compassionate approach allowed room for me to apologise and make amends, or do better next time (or hopefully both!).

Her phrase, "That's not like you," reminded us kids that she loved us and knew we were better than our behaviour in that moment. It encouraged us to do better.

Learning how to stop being a chameleon and actually speak my truth meant embracing and practicing new skills in communication and conflict resolution. It meant being honest with myself about how I was feeling and finding a way to communicate that to others in a way that brought us closer together rather than pushing us apart.

I'm by no means an expert on the art of human communication *(any day now!)*, but one thing that has helped me to get through a conflict or conversation without having a heart attack is to ask myself some probing questions before approaching the conversation. For example, what do I really want out of this discussion? Am I leading with love and approaching this person in a way that will unite us, or am I simply trying to shame, blame, or control?

Oof, I know. This is a big one, right? Asking and answering this question takes humility, courage, and a deep level of honesty. Do you simply want to prove you're right? Do you want to fight for the position of the biggest victim in the conflict, somehow proving to them you've been hurt the most, thereby guilting them into something? Or do you genuinely want to clear the air so your relationship will be all the stronger for it moving forward?

What's the big picture outcome you're hoping for? If someone's hurt you, what do you want the future to look like with them, and how could you talk with them about it in a way that makes them more inclined to get onboard with this vision as well?

As you broach the subject, figure out the real problem. Endeavour to understand the other person's point of view. Ask them questions to really try and see things from their perspective. Why did they react the way they did? Why do they feel so strongly about this issue? What do *they* hope the big picture outcome will be?

If you're in a disagreement with a friend or family member over a plan, is there a compromise you could work on, rather than simply expecting each other to give in to the other's demands?

Having a clear desired outcome in your mind before you speak can help keep you focused on resolving the conflict in a way that ensures everyone feels heard and respected. If the discussion goes off a on a tangent, try to calmly bring the focus back to the proposed solution. It'll help you to remain patient and positive.

Another tool that can help with this is to practice extending your reaction time. That is, to breathe and wait for a beat before responding. *Oh my,* how I struggled with this one. Blame the fiery Aries star sign I was born under, or simply my fear that I wouldn't get the chance to speak my piece, keeping a cool and steady head was a skill I had to learn and practice.

As a kid, I spent a lot of time together with my sister and cousins at my grandparent's house. We were a ragtag gaggle of four who were always getting up to mischief. We never intended for any of us to get into trouble, of course, but kids being kids, we often did. Often we'd be knee-deep in some kind of hijinks only to hear my Uncle's voice booming across the room, *"WHO DID THIS?!"*

Four sets of eyes widened in horror before we all started babbling, "Well um kinda all of us but we had this great plan see this thing was supposed to happen but then this thing went wrong and..."

"STOP!" My Uncle would bellow, never a man to suffer fools gladly. "Think before you speak!"

I thought this was such an odd request at the time. Why wouldn't you just want us to tell you what happened as quickly as possible? *What were we waiting for?*

My cousins and I would all look at each other like, *huh?*

When my Uncle indicated it was my turn to explain my version of events, rather than thinking before I spoke, I simply spoke more slowly in order to appease him.

It was only as I watched those reality shows that I saw how the people who flew off the handle and shouted over each other never seemed to get their differences resolved, whereas the ones who slowed down and really listened to the other person before communicating tended to walk away with a stronger level of mutual understanding. Or, at the very least, the peace and self-esteem that came with knowing they tried their best.

Another big question that can help to reframe it, is what is this conflict or situation here to teach me? The fact is, we're all human, trying to figure things out. We all have our own fears and worries, preconceptions and priorities. We all mess up sometimes, and we all bene-fit from compassion. The relationships in our lives are here for our learning and healing. What are yours here to teach you?

I've always loved sayings like, "The Universe won't always give you what you want, but it will always give you what you need." Challenging situations and rela-tionships offer us even more lessons and personal growth.

Of course, having a sense of humour never goes astray. I always love to think of Jerry Seinfeld in his self-titled sitcom. No matter what the conflict was - no matter if his best friend had damaged his car or his neighbour had eaten every last thing in his fridge - he rarely let his anger or emotions get the better of him. He almost always kept his sense of humour, and rather than yelling, was more curious about the expla-nations and motivations of others. Keeping a cooler head helped him to more clearly explain why he wasn't happy with their behaviour and what he expected of them in future.

Often if Dom and I have a conflict that I didn't handle as well as I would have liked, my sheepish apology later includes the words, "I'm sorry. I had a sense of humour failure." Finding the humour in my reaction always helps me to apologise. It helps me to lighten the load, and remember not to take myself so seriously next time. Sometimes it's a matter of picking your battles or deciding if this is really the hill you want to die on.

The thing is, we'll all have conflict in our lives. Unless we choose to live alone in the wilderness, we always will. We can therefore spare ourselves a lot of heartache if we trust that the other person is either trying to show love (to us or someone else), or is crying out for love.

If all else fails, breathe. Escape to another room, go for a walk around the block, take a nap, indulge in some radical self-care.

If a situation doesn't improve, you may have to create some distance in that relationship because being around them is not healthy for you. Whether they make you feel badly about yourself, zap your energy, or repeatedly disrespect or double-cross you, toxic relationships are bad for us and everyone around us.

Remember, when you're resolving conflict, it's not your responsibility to save anyone from the awkwardness that comes with clearing the air. Resist the urge to fix or rescue the other person.

Dom is such a great role model to me in this area. Whenever we go shopping, whatever store we happen to find ourselves in, he feels completely at ease smiling and asking the shop assistant, "What's your best price?"

There's a mild conflict there, of course: the salesperson wants to sell the item at a higher price (and make a higher commission); the customer wants to buy the item at a lower price (and save themselves money).

Dom's more than happy to wait for as long as it takes for the assistant to stutter and stammer their way to an answer, never once feeling the urge to jump in and relieve them of the awkwardness. Meanwhile, I was always over there in the corner attempting not to hyperventilate.

It's not your job to make anyone feel less awkward, especially if it involves betraying yourself in the process.

When I think back to all the times I've jumped in to try to 'save' someone, I can barely think of an example of when the other person seemed grateful or relieved I did so. Again, I'm assuming that they feel awkward because I do. It's possible they're just taking their time considering and communicating their answer. Perhaps they even enjoy a bit of healthy tension. *Who knows?* I can't read their thoughts.

And if all of this is true, am I jumping in simply to relieve my *own* awkwardness? Or am I trying to win them over; demonstrating myself to be 'nice', thereby trying to ensure they like me? Could I instead lean into that discomfort a little more, and see what revelations await me in the pause?

It's not your responsibility to make others feel comfortable in a discussion; it's theirs.

If you're still terrified to have a conversation in person, you could try writing notes first, or writing a letter to them instead. Use whatever communication method you can. If you're not comfortable asking for your needs to be met face-to-face, you might like to call the person, or send an email. Sometimes we can better articulate our thoughts when we thoughtfully write them out first.

When I was a teenager and was upset with a friend, I always wrote them a letter in which I poured my heart out about why I was hurt by what they'd done and how much I loved them and wanted to resolve things. I never posted a single one of those letters. And yet, somehow things always shifted after I penned them.

At the time I thought it was some kind of magic, but now I realise it was probably my energy that changed as I approached them after that. I'd gotten the big picture clear in my mind; I'd remembered that our relationship was bigger than our squabble. We cared about each other. And because of that, somehow - whether in my energy or my facial expressions or my words - I was making room for them to apologise, and for us to reach a new level of understanding.

As long as you communicate honestly and respect-fully, it's okay to use whichever method you're most comfortable with. You don't have to be vulnerable before you're ready. But it's true that every time we practice better communication skills in person, face-to-face, we get better at them, and our confidence grows. Which means we're much more capable of communi-cating like a grown-up the next time the salsa hits the fan.

Believe me, I'm still learning and growing in these skills every day. It's rarely easy, but it's always worth it. Each time we're assertive whilst also being kind, it gets that little bit easier. Every time we lead with love and resolve a dispute, we build our self-esteem and deepen the relationships we most care about.

Conflict is a portal to a new level of trust and understanding in our relationships, and clear communication is the vehicle that can get us there.

13. Ditching Disrespect

I was about fourteen the first time I wrote in my diary: "NEVER. TRUST. ANYONE."

I scrawled it across the page in large letters and underlined it five times, just to really drive the message home.

I don't remember if it was a friend or a boy who'd disappointed me enough to inspire that writing session. I don't know if the notion was instilled in me during my parent's divorce when I was eight, or the challenges of switching schools three times before I was ten. But I do remember the heart of those words: People will betray you. People let you down, or leave you. People break your heart.

For as long as I can remember, I've been fiercely independent and self-reliant. I often didn't know what I was doing, mind you, and my emotional maturity and bravado were often that of a teenager even when I was much older, but I wasn't shy in the face of taking action.

I started my first part-time job when I was thirteen. I rented my own apartment by the time I was eighteen. I moved to London by myself when I was twenty-three and stayed for three years, before moving to Sydney; another city where I started completely from scratch. In my late thirties, I switched careers from the project management path I'd been on for two decades in the corporate world, to the relative uncertainty and mayhem of working for myself as a creative entrepreneur and health coach.

I was curious and courageous in many ways, and that independence served me well in accumulating life experiences. But when it came to relationships, that ultra independence also meant that I held people at arm's length. I was scared to let people get too close, and I never, ever asked anyone for help. With anything. *Perish the thought!*

See, if I never put myself in a situation where I relied on someone, I'd never have to be disappointed when they didn't show up for me, or when they dropped the ball. If I did everything myself, I only had myself to blame.

In other words, my extreme independence was a preemptive strike against heartbreak. It was a trust issue. I didn't trust anyone else not to let me down, and I didn't trust myself, either, to choose people.

Trust involved vulnerability, and hope. And from

what I'd seen, every relationship went downhill at some point. Friends were flaky. Boyfriends were lovely, at first.

I've had three serious, long-term relationships in my life. In the first two, there was always a point where our relationship shifted from pure love and sexy joy to… well, something else. I had no idea what this turning point was, or why it kept happening to me. I figured it was just what happens with men: at some point, they stop being kind and romantic and fun, and instead speak to their partners like they just stepped in dog poo. Either that, or they completely neglected or took them for granted.

I had no clue that I played any real part in this scenario at all. It was only with Dom, in our first year of living together, that I started to gain an inkling that I might have had a bigger part to play in the cracks that appeared in my previous relationships.

Years ago, I watched a reality TV show called *Tough Love*, about a Relationship Coach hired to give a group of women a dose of truth medicine when it came to their dating behaviour. One woman in particular had a habit of drinking too much and making a fool of herself in front of her dates. Frustrated with witnessing this pattern of behaviour time and again, the host finally yelled, "How can you expect anyone else to love and respect you, if you don't love and respect *yourself?!*"

It was a sentiment I'd heard before, of course, but something about the way he said it, and the context in which it was said, meant it tumbled around my head for days. I thought about my internal monologue and how critical I always was of myself and my body. I noticed my unhealthy addictions to sugar, social media - and most especially - to alcohol. I squirmed as I observed my habit of people-pleasing for fear of being rejected, and the multitude of ways I let myself down and broke promises to myself. Could it be that all these patterns were merely symptoms of a dysfunctional relationship with *myself*?

As I began my quest of sobriety and self-discovery, I discovered that when we say things like: "When I find that perfect job/partner/friend (or in my case, "when *he* starts acting better"), *then* I'll be happy," we give our power away. The truth is, the most important and powerful relationship we will ever have is with ourselves. *Everything* else - all of our other relationships, fulfilment, creativity, health and happiness - first flow from there.

What if you spoke kindly to yourself, forgave your mistakes, followed your heart, encouraged your dreams, cheered yourself on, made your wellness a priority, and believed you could do it? How would that play out in the rest of your life? How would it permeate your relationships, boost your energy levels and self-belief, and ultimately help you reach for your dreams?

Really think about that with me for a minute. Because we weren't designed to stay small. We were created to stretch, to try new things, and to reach our beautiful potential. To follow our hearts, always, even when it's scary. To learn what love truly means and to practice it with everyone in our lives, starting with ourselves.

I know that's much easier said than done. Learning to love ourselves unconditionally is a long and winding journey. It encompasses self-trust (repairing the relationship with yourself), self-care (parenting yourself), self-worth and self-esteem (feeling good about yourself), and self-belief and self-confidence (trusting in your abilities).

For me, it also involved learning how to respect myself. This was the part that had damaged my romantic relationships the most. This was the weakness that had caused me, countless times, to make a fool of myself in front of colleagues at work functions.

I'm still haunted by one particular weekend when I lived in London. After a night out with a bunch of my colleagues, I woke up on Saturday morning with no memory of leaving the pub or how I got home. Small flashbacks of the night blinked through my head, but try as I might, I couldn't piece together the rest.

All weekend long, my imagination tormented me. Every minute of every hour, my stomach churned each time I thought about what I might have said or done.

As I hauled my sorry ass into the office on Monday, I felt sick with dread, praying I hadn't been the drunkest one at the function. Moving as fast as my fear and anxiety would allow, I sheepishly attempted to sneak to my desk unnoticed in our open plan office.

It was no use.

Instantly, six of the colleagues closest to me stood

up. Facing me with the wry grins on their faces that only Brits can do so well, they each gave a long, slow clap. Hearing the commotion, another three guys came around the corner to join in.

I was mortified. My body was blushing so hard it felt like I was on fire. I slumped into my chair and busied myself switching on my computer, desperately pretending I didn't notice what was happening, while I avoided meeting anyone's gaze. I didn't know whether to poop my pants, throw up, or burst into tears.

Finally, from the corner of my eye, I saw my closest work friend wave the others away.

"You alright?" he asked, his voice gentle, after the clapping had stopped. "We were only having a laugh."

I pulled my face into a weak smile and nodded, still staring directly at my computer screen in an attempt to avoid looking at him.

Sitting down and leaning across our desks so that only I could hear, he said quietly, "What happened to you on Friday? When you drink, it's like you're a completely different person."

I bit my lip and shrugged. I had absolutely no idea what had happened on Friday and I was far too humiliated and ashamed to ask. But I did know one thing. When I looked at the people I admired and respected, I was fairly damn sure none of them drank themselves silly or made a fool of themselves in front of the people they worked with every day. None of them threw their respect away like it was cheap confetti.

Kind friends would always wave away my drunken

antics with sweet comments of: "It's *fine*, babe. We've all been there." But it was in my lover's eyes that I could see it. It was in the workplace that I felt it. No wonder they didn't really respect me; they could see I didn't respect *myself.*

Once, when I was fifteen or so, my Mum's boyfriend at the time was driving me somewhere; possibly to pick her up from work. Neither of us spoke a word in the car. To be honest, I didn't really like this guy very much, and certainly not enough to trouble myself to come up with polite conversation.

We drove in awkward silence for the longest while. Suddenly, out of nowhere, he spoke. "You don't respect me, do you?"

In a heartbeat, without thinking, I said: "You have to *earn* respect."

In that moment, I had no idea where it came from. It was such a grown-up thing to say, and not like me at all. I didn't even really know what it meant. But somehow it had come out of the deepest depths of me. Somehow I knew it to be true.

Learning to respect myself felt like that same concept: of earning it. It happened as I made my bed each morning, and dressed in well-fitting clothes that made me feel good. It took place each time I decluttered my environment, and found a new way to keep myself organised. It showed up in every conversation where I chose my words carefully and was honest and up-front about my true feelings.

Each action - each time I did something I was

proud of - I built my self-respect. Every time I chose the harder option over something that was immediately comfortable or easy, I grew. And each time I upheld my boundaries, I taught others how to respect me. I modelled it in how I treated myself.

People mistakenly think that loving or caring for yourself is selfish: as though it's not directly linked to your capacity to love and care for others. The funny thing about taking care of yourself and learning to love yourself is that you're ready, willing, and able to give more generously to others: you *want* to, because your self-love is spilling over.

When you fill your cup first, you can give freely from the overflow: you can offer to help out of the goodness of your heart, with clean, healthy, abundant energy. It makes you feel warm and fuzzy, not exhausted, cranky, or resentful. You have more love and energy to give back to those around you.

When we don't allow others to help us, we're denying someone else that same joy. We all need other humans, and reaching out to help each other - and be helped - is one way to strengthen our connection and relationships.

What I wrote in my diary that fateful day when I was fourteen (and sadly, many days after that) was misguided. It wasn't that other people couldn't be trusted. It was that I needed to establish healthy boundaries that would allow me to give my whole heart whilst also caring for it. I needed to model my own self-respect and ensure that others also respected it. I needed to love myself up so I felt worthy of asking for, and receiving, help when necessary, and knowing I'd be completely okay if it didn't all go according to plan.

I needed to trust that I'd be safe, even in my vulnerability, precisely because I always, always had my own back.

This strength and safety is what awaits you in your own self-trust too. When you respect yourself and your decisions, you can choose how to respond if or when someone hurts you or lets you down. Sometimes you might need to more clearly communicate the types of behaviour that are, and aren't, okay with you. Other times it might be that the other person is simply struggling with something that feels insurmountable and you feel compelled to show them compassion and understanding.

Trusting yourself means understanding that you'll choose the right response for you in the moment. And that, if you don't, you have the ability and wisdom to choose again.

You feel free to trust others because you know that ultimately, you trust yourself. Even if they mess up, you'll still be here, caring for your heart and loving yourself, no matter what.

Your safety is in your self-love.

14. Tune in and Trust

Did you ever see the movie, 'I Feel Pretty'? If not, don't worry, I won't give you any spoilers, but it starts out with a woman who struggles on a daily basis with insecurity, low self-esteem, and feeling like she's failing at life.

Something happens (again, no spoilers) and just like *that*, in a single moment, it's like she becomes a completely different person. Suddenly she has *swagger*. She starts kicking goals at work, talking to people she'd never had the nerve to before, and asking out cute guys.

The curious part? Her looks, job, and situation are all exactly the same as they were before.

The one and only thing that changed? Her thoughts and beliefs.

For the first time, she believes she is beautiful and capable. She has complete confidence in her abilities and her potential. She thinks like a happy, self-assured, successful person.

Her thoughts and beliefs completely change her behaviour. She *becomes* those things (clever, captivating, confident) simply because she *believes* she is.

I loved this so much because I was totally on board with the message. Our thoughts are so powerful. We are what we eat, and we are what we think.

Perception is a selective act of attention and interpretation. What you experience as 'reality' is completely shaped by your choice of perception.

Say, for example, I went to a concert and absolutely loved it. The music moved my soul, the costumes and set captured my imagination, and I couldn't stop raving about it for weeks. Say my friend, however, went to the very same concert on the same night and hated it. The band didn't play her favourite song, or the bass gave her a headache, or it just didn't match her expectation of what she thought it would be.

The concert was exactly the same. The only thing that differed was our perception of the event; our opinions, and our unique interpretation of 'reality'.

It's precisely because of this that I love an affirmation that I first heard from Author Gabby Bernstein: *"I choose to see this differently"*. This little mantra helps me to remember that I always hold the power of my perception. No matter what happens, I can choose to focus on the good in the situation, find the silver

lining, and ask what I could learn from the experience. It reminds me that I'm always in control of my
thoughts; not the other way around.

And oh boy, did I use this touchstone a lot when
I first embarked on my sobriety path. Cultivating
a positive mindset helped me to focus on *why* I was
embarking on such a challenging journey at all, and
all the amazing things I was going to experience as a
result. It helped me to reframe sobriety as a new chap-
ter; a new adventure, rather than a lesson in torture.
Using affirmations and repetition helped me to focus
on the bigger picture, rather than the fact that I wasn't
going to drink that night or any night after that.

With enough time and practice, rather than dissolv-
ing into a sobbing fit on the kitchen floor, it became
natural for me to focus on solutions rather than prob-
lems. When someone now comes to me flustered with
an issue and requests my help, my favourite response
is, "Okay, let's see how can we solve that. What are our
options?"

Choosing to focus on options and solutions never
fails to make me feel more empowered. It boosts my
confidence and reminds me to think more creatively.
It assures me that we can figure out the best way to
handle any issue, so long as we stay focused on working together towards a resolution. It reminds me I can
always choose to take my thoughts, and my power,
back.

Another mantra I love is: "I choose to believe…".
This is such a great prompt that has the power to

rapidly change my thoughts and overcome anxiety spikes. Whenever I find myself feeling nervous or worried about something (usually because, once again, I'm making up a story about it in my head), these four little words help deliver me back to the present moment and remind me that I have ultimate control of the thoughts rolling around in my mind.

Rather than my old fearful cry of "But what if...", I choose to believe the situation is simpler and less dramatic than I'm making it out to be. I choose to believe they haven't emailed me back yet simply because they're busy this week.I choose to believe tomorrow will be easier.I choose to believe that person was cranky with me because they're secretly going through a hard time; it wasn't personal. I choose to believe I am bold, and brave, and the next time I approach a difficult conversation or situation, I will be even better at it.

Practicing gratitude daily is also a great way to train your mind to focus on the positive. Gratitude has the capacity to shift our awareness and personal reality, changing our approach to others and the world. And when we shift our beliefs, feelings, and attitudes, we shift our life! Gratitude empowers us to see the opportunities in our life with fresh eyes.

One of my favourite parts of each day is to write in a small journal that I keep in my bedside table. Every night I write just a sentence or two about my favourite or happiest moment from that day: small, simple things that made me smile.

Granted, sometimes it can take me a while to think

of things to write, but once I get started, I feel infinitely better. Even on those tough, emotional days when it feels like nothing is going my way, I challenge myself to see my day with a different perspective and write down at least one thing I'm grateful for. It's such a simple practice, but one that really helps to shake me out of everyday worries, and focus on what matters most: the little opportunities we have every day to truly see the beauty and meaning in life. Not to mention, getting me into a much more peaceful place before bed, which helps no end with my sleep!

I know the practice of gratitude may sound overly simplistic or trite, especially when you're going through extremely tough circumstances, but it really is such an easy, peaceful, and loving way to clear our minds before sleep, or to greet each new day.

It's also an activity the whole family can do together. You could keep a notebook, write on little slips of paper that you collect in a jar to read later, or take a photo per day of something that brought you joy.

Another powerful way to detox negative thoughts is through meditation. It's like a bubble bath for your mind. Of course, we know meditation is great for managing stress, but the thing I love most about it, is how it also helps you to tune into your intuition.

I'll be honest, when people used to say: "Listen to your gut" or "Follow your intuition" I'd politely smile and nod along, pretending I knew what the hell that even meant. The truth was, I didn't have a clue. I'd spent the better part of two decades drowning out that tiny, friendly voice inside me, and I had no idea how to get it back. My drinking years had severely damaged my self-trust, and it was a long, slow process to repair that part of my relationship with myself.

Whenever I received an invitation, I immediately jumped to dreaming up all the reasons I *should* go, listing them in long, boring detail to Dom.

"Hold up," Dom often said, clearly seeing straight through all of my nonsense. "Forget all that. What does your gut say?"

No matter how many times we had this conversation, I'd stare at him blankly until he tried the question again. "What was your initial reaction?"

"Well…" I considered, on too many occasions to count. "I guess my first instinct was dread."

And there it was. Pure honesty from deep inside my own unique bundle of personality traits and preferences. Before my mind had a chance to rationalise or create a list of expectations as to what I *should* do, my intuition had given me my answer. It always did. It was always there. I just had to slow down enough to tune in.

Logical thought rarely held the true answer for me; my intuition did.

The antidote to being a pushover is emotional maturity and unwavering self-trust, including intuition and clarity. It's vital, therefore, as we begin to consciously choose our thoughts and tune into our intuition, that we become avid protectors of our mindset and energy.

I used to be terrible at this. I wasn't selective at all in the information sources I consumed, which meant that, as a sensitive bunny, I would read or watch things that would send me spiralling into despair, often for *days*. Each time I'd lose all sense of self as I relived the awful or toxic thing I'd seen or heard, over and over again.

Think of your brain as a super computer. If you program rubbish in, you're gonna get rubbish out! And oh *brother*, do we take in a ton of rubbish disguised as information each day in the digital age.

Where is your information coming from? Think about the TV shows you watch; the news stations or podcasts you listen to; the social media accounts you follow. Start to notice and question whether each source is actually helping you to help yourself or others. Be discerning and feel free to consciously unfollow negative or toxic people, shut down your social media accounts temporarily or permanently, stay off miserable forums, switch off overly sensationalised 'news' shows, or anything else that might derail your thoughts or mess with your anxiety levels or mindset.

Learning to like and show love for ourselves, and growing in confidence, requires an unlearning of all the negative thought processes that got us here in the first place. Think about it: if your best friend or sister was actively trying to make huge changes or improvements in her life, would you plonk her down in front of a nasty website, a bunch of ads that tell her she's not good enough just as she is, or even the nightly news? No way! You instinctively know that she needs to be nurtured and encouraged. That she needs positive, inspiring input in order to follow through on her goals and change her life for the better.

Find out what it feels like to become your own best friend. Read great books; watch inspiring TED talks or interesting documentaries; listen to uplifting podcasts and music. Learn, ponder, dream. Let this positive, constructive input inspire you into action, rather than sending you and your thoughts nose-diving.

This may also mean you need to avoid toxic or negative people until you feel mentally strong enough to handle them. Properly caring for yourself means protecting your mind and your energy.

Avoiding these people can be more difficult when they sit right next to you at work or are your own flesh and blood, of course, but look for ways to minimise contact with them. The everyday ups and downs in your own life are enough to deal with. You don't need additional theatrics to worry about, or nutty drama that isn't even your own.

Likewise, as you begin to choose your thoughts, choose your words carefully. Judging, gossiping, or criticising yourself or others will only ever make you feel worse. All words have power, even the ones whispered behind someone's back (or said to yourself inside your own head). Before you speak, consider the old adage: *Is it true? Is it kind? Is it necessary?*

When you're going through something especially

tough or heartbreaking, protecting your thoughts and energy is even more important. It can help to practice self-kindness every day, speaking to yourself with compassion like you would to a small child who feels lost, scared, or alone. Find mantras or affirmations that really resonate with you and say them aloud to yourself or write them on notes and stick them around your home. Surround yourself with love.

Naturally, consciously choosing our words also involves *keeping* our word. When I was drinking, I broke promises to myself over and over again. I told myself I'd only have one drink, and then I'd have seven. I swore black and blue that I'd only drink on two nights this week, and then I'd drink on four. I looked at myself in the mirror as I got ready for each party and promised I wouldn't get messy that night, only to end up in a sloppy, dishevelled heap.

Sound familiar? You might have experienced this cycle of making and breaking promises to yourself when it came to your diet, exercise regime, online shopping budget, or time spent scrolling on social media.

This kind of constant breaking of our word means we lose trust and belief that we'll ever follow through on *anything* we say we'll do. *Of course* we don't trust our intuition; we don't trust anything about ourselves.

So much of rebuilding self-trust comes through keeping your promises. Practice being impeccable with your word. If you say, "I'll do it tomorrow," make sure you do! So much joy and self-esteem await us in the follow-through. This one simple act of keeping your word can allow you to get to know, like, and trust yourself again. Do what you say you're going to do. Be where you say you'll be.

Of course, this may take a ton of practice. Years ago I had a friend who had a habit of rarely turning up when she said she would. She was a beautiful person and a good friend in so many ways, but her people-pleasing tendencies meant she said yes to everything and then flaked at the last minute when she received a more pressing invitation or was exhausted from an overpacked schedule.

I thought it was only me who felt disappointed whenever I arrived at an event she said she was coming to (which was quite possibly the whole reason I was going in the first place), only to receive a text saying she wasn't going to make it. But on one such occasion, another friend received the same text message and exclaimed, "*Ugh!* What is her *deal?* She's so flaky! I'm going to tell her that right now!"

Our friend's people-pleasing habits had completely backfired, leaving her with a reputation that she couldn't be trusted to keep her word.

Your subconscious feels like that too. Shaking off that reputation of being a flake is a process of practicing keeping your word over and over again.

When you promise yourself you'll go to the gym, or finish a creative project, or anything else that is important to you, keep your promise to yourself. Your promise to yourself is just as important, if not more, as any promise you make to anyone else. Don't allow others to steamroll you into doing what they want you to do. Bravely resist abandoning yourself.

When others ask you for help, slow down your yes. As people like to say in the business world: underpromise and overdeliver. Or in this case, promise less so you *can* deliver. Only commit to doing things or attending events that mean something to you and that you know you have the capacity to follow through on.

Of course, sometimes life happens. Your baby gets sick; your car breaks down; your bathroom tap springs a leak. But keeping your word as much as possible will not only show others they can rely on you, it'll also prove to yourself that you always have your own back.

15. Esteemable Acts

Many years ago when I was in the corporate world, my work friend, Rose, bought a new camera. It was a fairly nice model, with lots of bells and whistles, that she planned to use to capture better family and holiday photos. Keen to better understand how to use it, when the camera store invited her to a class dedicated to learning beginner tips and tricks, she decided to enrol.

Rose showed up to that class with zero expectations; simply a willingness to follow her curiosity. In the first class, she felt a little out of her depth but trusted that if she at least learnt the basics, she'd be able to get more out of her new purchase. So she turned up at the second class, and then the third. And somewhere along the way, something magical happened. Rose fell in love with taking photos.

These days she's travelling on photography safaris, winning regional awards, and seeing her beautiful photos presented in galleries. Rose is in her sixties and had absolutely no idea that this talent and passion had been hidden within her all this time.

I love this so much I can barely tell you. If there's one thing guaranteed to boost our confidence and help us build a strong sense of self, it's getting progressively better at something. Whether we build, make, or learn something, when we create rather than consume, we get a sense of self-satisfaction and joy that no amount of shopping, scrolling, or binge-watching can ever provide.

Despite what we may have been told by marketing companies for decades, it's growth that generates happiness. It's action that creates confidence.

Discovering hidden talents or passions within ourselves is not only a heap of fun, it also brings wonder back to our lives. It makes us feel good about ourselves. It allows us to embrace more of who we truly are and what lights us up, even if we're not entirely sure what that is at the time.

A few years ago, when a friend casually mentioned he was going to Scandinavia, Dom and I became enchanted with the idea of joining him on a grand adventure.

"Wow, we have to go hiking!" Dom said when he saw photos of beautiful Norway.

"Hiking?" I scoffed. "I don't *think* so! There are lots of other adventures that don't involve hiking!"

You see, I'd been down that road before, my friend. When I was in my mid-twenties, a friend and I back-packed around South Africa. In one town, we booked a tour that promised to take us "to the top of the summit".

We thought they meant in a *bus*.

The next morning, when our tour bus stopped halfway up the incline, we were flabbergasted. In our hungover state, we hadn't read the fine print.

As our guide explained that we'd be walking the rest of the way up, I'll admit, I was *pissed*.

It'd been raining the day before, so in my ridiculous shoes, it was just a matter of time before I slipped and ended up with mud all over my backside. At our lunch break, I bit into a hard-boiled lolly and broke a tooth. I mean, *what on earth?* I don't remember ever breaking a tooth in my life, but for some reason I had to break one halfway up a flippin' *mountain?*

I was in pain and humiliated and couldn't wait for the whole day to be over so I could sink my hangover back into another glass of wine.

You can see why I wasn't exactly thrilled to try hiking ever again. But the Universe had other plans.

When I messaged my beautiful Norwegian friend that we were coming to her homeland, the first thing she wrote back was, "Oh my God, I can't wait, I'll take you to all the best hiking spots!"

You should know, at this point in the story, that my friend hikes huge mountains for fun. She run marathons and has completed multiple-day walking endeavours across the Australian desert, simply to challenge herself. She's a beautiful force of nature, and one of the strongest, fittest, and bravest women I've ever known.

It was precisely because of this that upon reading her reply, my very first thought was, "Oh my God, *I'm going to die!*"

I was *this* close to writing back and telling her there was no way in hell this kooky plan was going to happen. I was not hiking, not in this lifetime, *no siree Bob!*

But as I looked at the photos she'd sent me of her favourite hiking spots, I had to admit it looked stunning. As scared as I was of the idea, a small sense of excitement began to take hold. I didn't know if I'd like the experience, but I was curious enough to find out.

Then it occurred to me: I was no longer that drinking twenty-something. I was different now. I was a different person, and I could absolutely become a hiker if I put my mind to it.

Instead of running from the opportunity, I decided to wholeheartedly embrace it! Dom and I renewed our gym memberships and spent the next few months training our bodies to be stronger for the climb. Each week I watched my strength and stamina improve, just a little bit. And when I boarded the plane to Scandinavia, I felt proud of myself for even attempting something so bold.

When it came to the morning of the hike, sure, I was nervous. As we drove up to the base of the mountain and stared up at the top, the climb felt like an impossible pipe dream. But over the course of the next few hours, I actually *did* it! One step at a time. Hundreds of steps of crazy, rocky terrain to climb to the top. My very first real hike.

What I didn't expect was just how much I would fall in love with it. All of it. The oversized hiking boots, the fresh air, the sunshine, the smell of the trees, and the pure exhilaration of the challenge. It was so much harder than I thought it would be - my muscles ached like mad, my hair and face were a mess, and I stank more than I ever had in my life - but it was also infinitely more rewarding. And I felt like a total badass because this kind of active living was something I never thought I could do, or the type of person I could be.

The most powerful part about trying new things is that every time we challenge ourselves and succeed, we push the boundaries of what we previously believed was possible. We learn, grow, and gain more confidence and faith that we can handle the next hard thing. We feel better about ourselves, and that pride and confidence spills over into our relationships. We start standing up for ourselves, and being more protective of the time we want to pour into the things we enjoy.

Not to mention opening our eyes to what's possible. I *never* thought I could ever have fun on a sober holiday, never mind be a person who hiked; not as a matter of survival but simply for the joy of it! Developing authentic confidence is a journey into rediscovering who you truly are and what lights you up.

When we feel stuck or bored with life, or lacking in confidence, it's often because we don't have something to look forward to or work towards. When we're training for something (like a hiking trip), developing a new skill (like photography), taking up a new series of classes, or working on a passion project, we feel excited about a future filled with possibilities.

Watching our progress - noticing that we get just that little bit stronger, better, or more educated each day - can bring a sense of fulfilment and more joy and meaning to our lives. We begin to accumulate a wealth of evidence that shows we're actually good at certain things; or, at the very least, have the tenacity to hang in there as we improve at them.

As they say: if you're not growing, you're dying.

That is, embracing *your* passions, not the passions your friends, family, or colleagues insist you should care about. Just as we're unique in our personalities, we're also unique in our passions, and the world is all the richer for it. It means we have people working on advancements in science, technology, and healthcare. It means we have people who volunteer at animal shelters and others who volunteer to bring meals to the elderly. It means we have people who make music, and others who paint masterpieces.

Your dreams and curiosities are as unique as your personality and quirks. They're what make you special. Embrace them. Follow where they lead you.

Discovering new things you're good at, and exploring stuff you're curious about, are just one way to boost your self-esteem, of course. Another method is through self-care, specifically 'adulting' *(oh no!)* when you don't really want to. Doing things like taking care of long-overdue medical appointments, resting when you need to instead of endlessly pushing yourself past your limits, and organising your finances. Actions that might feel scary in the moment but ultimately make you feel proud of yourself and build your self-esteem.

Man, did I get a crash course in this over the past few years.

As any previous drinker will tell you, whether you've been sober for a few days, months, or years, you're likely - at some point - to experience flash-backs. There you are, trucking along nicely - feeling good about yourself and actually *enjoying* your alco-hol-free ride - when suddenly, *BOOM!*, memories of past behaviour come flooding back.

I was having one of those moments. Or rather, I was having one of those weekends. I had no idea what had triggered it, but I felt steeped in shame, regret and sadness over events that had taken place years, if not decades, prior. As much as I tried to shake myself out of it, I was spiralling, and I was not enjoying it one little bit.

In the midst of this emotional shitstorm, my parents called, and during the conversation mentioned that a friend of the family was in a nearby hospital after suffering some health complications. Unfortunately, they were out of town for the week so they wouldn't be able to go visit her.

"Oh, that's a shame," I said, still partially caught up in my own mind melt melodrama.

It was only after I hung up the phone that it occurred to me how I'd often fallen into a kind of passive, child-like role in the family hierarchy. And now that I was a grown-ass woman attempting to expand in confidence and self-worth, perhaps I could step up to help.

"Mary's in the hospital," I told Dom. "I know it would mean a lot to my parents - and to her - if I went to visit. Want to come with me?"

"Sure," Dom agreed easily, and I loved him for it. "Let's go."

Now, I loved this family friend dearly, but I'd never spent any time with her one-on-one. This fact alone would have stopped me in the past. The fear that always tugged at my little introverted heart was, *what would we even talk about?*

I still had the same fear on the drive to the hospital, but rather than shove this worry down, I confided in Dom.

"Yeah," Dom said, nodding thoughtfully. "I guess if I think about it, I've always shied away from these kinds of things too. It's like a form of social anxiety; I wouldn't know what to say."

If you're a born extrovert, this might seem utterly bizarre to you, but when we're not that way naturally inclined, interacting with people can bring up all kinds of weirdness. Being honest with Dom about my feelings allowed me to exhale a little bit, and feel less nervous on the walk up to Mary's room.

The funny thing was, the moment we got there, all my nerves completely fell away. She was *thrilled* to see us, and we stayed for over an hour with not a moment's silence between us. It was a magical visit that she later told my parents meant so much to her, as it did to them.

But most of all, it meant a great deal to me. Not only did I feel infinitely closer to Mary, but it was also such a beautiful reminder that regardless of how bad I was feeling emotionally, I always had the power to do something that made me feel better about myself. Rather than wallowing in my pity party about things I couldn't change, I could shake off the haunted remnants of my past and take action to create the kind of present and future I can be proud of.

I know that historically, pride was generally considered to be a bad thing, often because it was wrapped up in beliefs about morality, conceit, vanity, and the ego. But in the vast majority of people I've had the honour of coaching and supporting, having too big of an ego was never the problem. In fact, it was quite the opposite. Too many of us, it seems, are immensely self critical, with phenomenally low self-esteem.

When we stop people-pleasing, embrace sobriety, or embark on a journey of personal development of any kind, the change in behaviour tends to come hand-in-hand with a change in identity and lifestyle, which inevitably is a great thing. But during the bumpy transition phase, many of us can find ourselves struggling with feelings of isolation, shattered self-image, and difficulty processing complicated emotions.

To feel proud of ourselves, then, is a completely foreign, new, and beautiful experience. One that helps to grow our self-worth and confidence.

When I first stopped drinking, I had a vague concept of what self-esteem was. I mean, I knew I didn't have enough of it. But I had no idea how, or where, to get more. I remember the first time I read, 'self-esteem comes from doing esteemable acts'. With that one little sentence and concept, the fog began to lift.

When I was drinking, I was often ashamed of myself and my actions. I didn't have a lot of experience with being *proud* of myself. Was it any wonder then that I looked to others for validation or approval?

By consciously rebuilding our self-worth and confidence, we're able to be true to ourselves and not allow others to steamroll us.

Your self-esteem will never come from others; it comes from *you*. It's a gift you can give yourself; a skill you can practice.

On days when emotions feel overwhelming, or I just can't seem to push through to the other side, I break it down to its simplest form. *What could I do to feel proud of myself today? What's one small action that would make me feel good about myself?*

Sometimes it's a larger task, but often it's as simple as making my bed, running a long-overdue errand, or eating a piece of fruit instead of more chocolate. For you, it might be performing a random act of kindness for a neighbour, taking responsibility for something in your life (like booking a dentist appointment or some other 'adulting' task you've been putting off), or doing something you're good at (like tending to your herb garden, baking a cake, or playing the piano).

Try doing something you're proud of every day. Find out how delicious it feels. Boost your self-esteem by doing something that makes you feel good; something that makes you say, "Hey, I did a really good job!" or "I'm so proud of myself for that," or "I'm so proud of the way I handled that" in relationships with others, or in doing things differently for the first time.

Every time you take action and do something that's good for you (*especially* the actions we feel the most resistance to, but know in our heart of hearts will be good for us), you boost your self-esteem. And because it feels so great, in turn it boosts your happiness levels and confidence, which means you're more likely to do it again!

In other words, action creates powerful momentum that you can build upon.

That simple question: *what could I do to feel proud of myself today?*, helps me to remember that we all do so much more each day than we give ourselves credit for.It helps to shake me out of a fear spiral or overwhelmed funk, and inspires me into action.It helps me to feel like I have some sort of control over my life and destiny, in a world of uncertainty. And most of all, it helps to remind me that we are all completely empowered. That we can continue to lift these tiny building blocks that stack up to feeling good about ourselves.

Go ahead, have a little brainstorm with me now. What's one small action you took (or could take) today that made you feel good about yourself? What's one thing you're proud of?

When Dom and I were planning our trip to Scandinavia, we started chatting about other things we might also like to experience on that trip. Dom suggested hiring bikes and riding out to the countryside, and I must admit, my reaction was much the same as when he first suggested hiking; something along the lines of: "*No!* I haven't been on a bike in more than a decade. I'm not the type of person who goes freakin' *cycling* on a trip. No way!"

But a funny thing happens when you do *one* brave thing (like, say, hiking, turning up to a new class, or meeting someone for a first date). It gives you confidence that you can conquer the *next* scary thing (like getting your derrière back on a bike for the first time in decades, or having that tricky conversation you've been avoiding).

Because, despite what my teenage-self believed, true confidence doesn't come from a bottle or from the approval of others. It comes from doing one brave thing after another and proving to yourself that you are capable of so much more than you ever believed possible.

Because you are. We all are. So. Much. More.

16. You Are Enough

I must admit, I've never been a natural at maths or languages. A few weeks into my first semester of eleventh grade, I decided that my choice of French class was going to be an uphill battle and that I'd much rather change my elective subject to Theatre Arts. I didn't know much about the theatre, but our school had just built a brand new performing arts complex, and as a kid I'd always loved making up musical plays and dance numbers in the privacy of my own bedroom, so I thought it sounded like fun.

As I rushed back from the Principal's office just in time to grab the seat next to my friend in History class, I excitedly whispered my new plan to her.

"Theatre Arts?!" she balked, her eyes goggling at me. "*What?* You can't! You're too shy!"

She wasn't entirely wrong. While I was relaxed and happy within my small group of friends, I had a tendency to clam up around new people, often leaving her to do all the talking.

"I know," I blushed and shrugged. "But it might be fun."

Part of me knew I had no business even having the gall to *think* I could do it, and yet there was another part, a more persistent little voice from within, that wanted to try. I was terrible at French and Calculus, and sports bored me to tears, but the creative stuff? Those subjects, I really enjoyed.

I'd already won awards in metal work, photography, and even art class, despite having no natural aptitude or experience in them. I was simply curious enough to find them interesting and fun, and it was this tiny seed of curiosity that inspired and enabled me to create something new and different.

My first theatre arts class will be forever etched into my memory. Rather than in the new performing arts complex, for some reason this class was held in an old, demountable classroom on the outskirts of school. It was hot and run down, and we had to push a heap of desks aside to make room for a little performing space.

After we'd finished shuffling the room around, our teacher announced that we'd be doing "an improv exercise". Okay, so I might not have been great at French, but I'd always thought I had a fairly good grasp on the English language. *Improv? Huh?*

I had no idea what that meant, but since I'd joined

the class a few weeks late, I figured I'd just hang around towards the back and watch everyone else until I figured it out. Little did I know our teacher was a big fan of the sink or swim method. I watched precisely *one* other improv exercise between two of our class-mates - the first one I'd ever seen in my life - before our teacher called on me.

As fate would have it, one of the most popular and confident girls in the entire school was in my class, and our teacher clearly thought it was a marvellous idea to match her with the new girl (yours truly), instructing us to perform an improvisation exercise in front of the entire class.

Aaahhh, improvise. That's what it meant. Oh God, no.

As I stood and walked to the front of the classroom, silently begging my knees not to give out beneath me, a boy towards the back yelled out, "Nice sideburns!"

A twitter of laughter echoed around the room as our teacher barked at them to keep it down.

I knew he couldn't possibly be directing an insult at The Goddess, which meant it was aimed squarely at me. Blushing a deep crimson I could feel to the tips of my toes, I awkwardly pushed my wayward, permed hair back behind my ears and attempted to calm myself. I could barely keep a conversation going in real life when it was just me and one other person I didn't know very well. How was I going to do this in front of an entire *audience*; and a hostile one at that?

Thankfully, the other girl was not only effortlessly

cool and self-assured, but also kind. As we locked eyes, I saw she'd made the decision to help. Either that, or she took one look at me and knew she was going to have to do most of the work. Either way, she took my one-word, spluttered answers and spun them into impressive performance gold that held the class spellbound.

As the final applause rang out and she took a little bow, I slumped back to my seat, positive I should quit right then and there. What was I even *thinking* coming into a class like this? I was never going to be as good as she was. I was so out of my league, and so close to marching straight up to head office to tell them I'd made a huge mistake and needed to switch again, but something stopped me.

What if this is as bad as it gets? I felt utterly freaked out the first time I rode a bike or started a part-time job, too, and yet, with enough practice, I managed to master them.

Yes, she was a million miles better than me and I might never be that good as hard as I tried for as long as I lived, but so what? I was allowed to have fun doing the best I could, right?

That one little thought kept me in the class. Throughout the next two years, as I developed my skills, there were always people who were infinitely better than me. I never scored the leading roles, or received any accolades for any of my performances, but none of that mattered. All that mattered was I had a blast. To this day, my best memories about high school are around theatre arts and the camps and performances and friendships I made there.

For better or worse, I'd always possessed a rich inner life; an imaginary dream world all of my own. So to find a place where we could make-believe and simply *play* all day felt like a dream come true. I didn't feel so shy there: it felt like a safe space to play dress-ups with all the other drama geeks. It was pure fun.

As adults, we often psyche ourselves out of trying new things for fear of not being good enough, or more specifically, not being as good as someone else. We often compare our beginning to someone else's middle or end.

Not all comparison is inherently bad, of course. Real Estate Agents compare houses in each neighbourhood to give you a fair estimate for yours. When we're in the market for a new car, we compare makes and models to figure out which one might be the best fit for our family and lifestyle. I often compare my creative writing to those I admire to see how I might improve.

We tend to call this kind of comparison, however, 'research' or 'inspiration'. We recognise it as having a fun, exciting energy to it, as opposed to regular old comparison that makes us feel like we don't quite measure up.

Remember when we didn't have social media or reality television? Remember when the only person you thought you needed to compete with was the most confident girl in your class; the one who won all the awards and had the cutest hair clips?

A whole new world opened up for us in the technology age, and not all of it is so crash-hot for our self-esteem. In the space of two short decades, our brains have all but exploded with the possibilities and exhaustion of trying to keep up with everyone else's highlights reels.

You tidy your garden and feel so great about it, you post a photo on social media… only to come across a photo of Jane, who's just remodelled her entire house, or Spencer, who's just received a prestigious award. Suddenly that warm, lovely feeling in your stomach is replaced by a shitty mood. Next to their achievements, yours doesn't feel nearly good enough. Heck, *you* don't feel good enough. All that self-worth, *POOF!* Gone in an instant.

Social media can be a breeding ground for 'comparisonitis', and a complete extinguisher of joy.

The only person you need to be better than is the one you were yesterday. Everyone is on their own journey. No two people have the same background, resources, or experiences, and therefore no two people ever run exactly the same race. There will always be someone who is smarter than you, or richer, or more successful, or who has a tidier garden. None of that takes away from what *you* have achieved. Everyone is swimming in their own lane, and running their own marathon. Stay focused on *you*; on your growth, your goals and achievements, your joy.

How exactly do we do this, you ask? By getting clear on the type of life you want to live, and doing more of what makes *you* happy and proud. Start by asking yourself the following questions: When you imagine yourself at ninety years old, reflecting back on your life and everything you've experienced, which accomplishments and milestones do you think will be the most important to you?

What kind of person do you hope to be? What kind of relationships do you want to have? What do you want people to remember about you?

Use these personal values as your yardstick for comparison, rather than the achievements or lives of others.

I once listened to a podcast interview with a woman who had a near death experience. As she talked about the experience after she flatlined and walked into the warm, welcoming light, she explained that it doesn't matter one bit to our soul or spirit - our life essence - what we do in our lives in comparison to others. All that matters is that we learnt our own lessons along the way.

I loved this so much because it feels so innately true: when we do things out of comparison or competition, they never feel as joyful or fulfilling as when we do something purely out of our own passion or curiosity. We only feel fulfilled and truly happy when we're following our own hearts.

Being enthralled with our smart phones and deeply entrenched in daily comparisons means it's sometimes hard to break the cycle and actually know what our hearts even want. Often I advise my coaching clients to shut down social media for at least thirty days. They resist this idea at first, of course. I did too. Our fear of missing out (also known as FOMO) can be just as strong as our Comparisonitis.

The first time I took a complete social media break, I literally had to force myself into it. Years ago, Dom and I spent a week on a remote island in Fiji that had zero internet access. Nada. Zip.

Oh boy, did the first few days of that trip really highlight how obsessive my phone checking compulsion had become. At least once an hour I'd see something cute and think, "Ooh, I'll share that!"... only to reach for my phone and experience a sinking sensation as the little 'no signal' icon taunted me from the top of the screen.

Whenever I felt a moment of boredom and wanted to see what everyone else was doing, I reached for it again. Still nothing.

The anxiety was unbearable. *What if people are trying to get hold of me? What's everyone doing out there? What if this awful feeling continues and ruins our entire trip?*

But once you push through those frustrating first few days, an incredible calm takes over. All that pressure is gone. You no longer have to keep up with The Joneses, or desperately 'prove' your worth. All the social 'noise' has been removed. Suddenly you're free to learn who *you* are and what *you* value most. It's liberating, delicious, and oh-so-expansive.

Forget what everyone else is doing. This lane - this

life - is for *you*. It's yours. You're far too unique to be compared to anyone else. You are you and that is your superpower. Give yourself the time, space, and energy to really get to know yourself again. Grant yourself that gift.

You are worthy of everything you dream of, and everything you want to try and experience in this life. You are enough, exactly as you are.

17. Practice Over Perfectionism

As I approached my seventeenth birthday (the legal age for driving in Australia), oh boy, was I excited to get my licence. I couldn't wait for the freedom and independence it would give me. I daydreamed for hours about zooming myself all over the city, heading to the beach after school, and driving off into the sunset on spontaneous road trips.

I knew it would be more difficult than learning how to drive an automatic, but I'd set my sights set on a manual car license so I had the skills to drive any and every vehicle I came across.

My Mum had generously promised she'd match me dollar for dollar on any car I chose, so I'd worked my butt off for months, working extra shifts at my part-time job until I had a thousand dollars saved. Oh I was so, so ready.

As per my usual mode of operation, I was far too impatient to do the recommended ten official lessons before my first exam. I'd already been for a few drives with my Mum's supervision, so I figured five oughta' do it.

I was brimming over with excitement and bravado, and as I rocked up to the licensing centre for my first driving test, I felt like nothing could stop me. *This was it!* I couldn't *wait* to tell my friends I'd finally have my own wheels!

Only, as the examiner climbed into the seat beside me and fastened his seatbelt, something strange happened. Instantly, all of my boldness evaporated. I was shocked and appalled to find I was a shaky, sweaty mess. Having someone sitting there, waiting to judge my every move, totally threw me off.

As I started the car and pulled out onto the street, I felt sick with the pressure to perform every manoeuvre perfectly. Each time the examiner silently scribbled notes on the score card pinned to his clipboard, I begged my arms, legs, and brain to remember what to do.

It was no use. About halfway through the exam, I sailed through a stop sign. *Ugh*, I know. Such a danger-ous, clichéd, rookie mistake, and an instant fail on the driving test.

So back to official lessons I went, with my sorry

tail between my legs, completing two more classes and giving extra focus to the art of stopping, even at 'Give Way' signs.

On the day I turned up for my second test, I was hopeful, but my anxiety was compounded. Now, I not only had fear of judgement but also a very real fear of failure. I mean, I had to get it on the second try, right? What kind of a loser fails twice?

This kind, as it turns out.

With a barrage of negative thoughts running through my head throughout the entire exam, I guess it shouldn't have come as any real surprise to me that my parallel parking was off.

Back to the lessons I went again, practicing my parking until I could turn any car on a dime.

When it came to my third test, I don't even remember what I did wrong, but I do remember feeling sick with shame that I *still* didn't leave with that bloody licence in my hand. My friend Sophie had taken several tests too, but she got her license on her third go. *What the hell was wrong with me?*

At home that night I sobbed for a good solid hour. Then I wiped away my tears and booked more lessons, determined to practice every possible driving skill until each one was etched deep into my muscle memory.

By the fourth test, something miraculous took place. As I climbed into the test car, I was astonished to find that my nerves and jitters had all but disappeared. For once, I didn't care what the examiner thought of me. I didn't feel the same energy of anxious desperation. Instead, I felt calm and self-assured.

Deep within me was a new understanding that I was going to keep coming back for these tests for as long as it took. My dream of my first car, and all the freedom it stood for, was far greater than my fear of failure. No matter if it took twenty tests, or fifty - no matter if the examiners *begged* and *pleaded* with me to stop coming - I was going to keep showing up, dammit!

An interesting thing happens when your energy shifts from wanting to please someone else (like an examiner) to focusing on your goal and understanding that you're willing to do whatever it takes to attain your dream. All the nervousness and external drama tends to fall away. In its place, a quiet confidence takes hold.

I knew I'd done everything I could: I'd practiced my little driving socks off. Now it was up to fate to decide if this would be the winning day, or if I'd still be showing up for tests when I was thirty-five. Either way, it was already decided; I wasn't going anywhere.

In a flash of pure irony, it was this calm, inner determination that gave rise to the best driving of my life. Parallel parking? *No problem.* Three point turn? *A cake walk.* The perfect speed and smoothest gear change on every street and every corner? *You got it.*

As the test came to its conclusion, we pulled back into the licensing centre and I stopped the car. Frowning, the examiner silently marked my score down on his tattletale little clipboard. I unlatched my seat belt and quietly sighed in resignation, waiting for his feedback and wondering what on earth the problem was this time. Whatever it was, I knew I'd get the hang of it eventually. I could take tests for the next twenty *years*; I wasn't giving up.

To my surprise, the examiner looked at me and smiled. "Almost a perfect score. Well done. That was the best driving I've seen all week."

I blinked at him, waiting for his words to register. *Holymacaroni*, I'd finally done it! I was a licensed driver at last, and I was thrilled.

The day I got my first car was one of the best of my young life. She was a second-hand, mustard yellow Datsun 120Y coupé, manufactured in 1977 and complete with a vanilla-scented deodoriser tree hanging from the rear view mirror. I named her 'Daisy' and she was *so* worth all the extra shifts I'd worked and every single driving test it took to get me there. Okay, so maybe she was a fifteen-year-old jalopy that struggled to make it up steep hills, and in certain light looked like the colour of newborn baby poop, but she was *all* mine; my personal freedom machine. I adored her.

That night, I hung out in my car for hours, revelling in the joy of having my own wheels at last, and the incredible feeling of pride and wonder in myself that I'd never given up.

I've received this lesson in various forms over the years. It never fails to surprise me, but whenever I release my vice-like grip on perfectionism, I actually have the most fun, and funnily enough, tend to be the most successful at whatever it is I'm trying to achieve.

This is such a funny anomaly because our drive for perfectionism tends to be rooted in our fear of failure, and yet it's this very attempt to do things perfectly can be precisely what leads to our downfall. Perfectionism can be an excellent and powerful tool for self-sabotage.

Perhaps even more bizarre is how scared we all are of failing. For me, the sense of shame that accompanied any perceived failure was deeply entrenched in what other people would think of me. I completely overlooked what failure would mean for my own sense of self-worth; for my growth and ultimate strength of character. I completely disregarded the fact that daring to fail means we were brave enough to try in the first place; that it speaks volumes about the strength and courage of our hearts.

The fact is, everyone makes mistakes. It doesn't mean we're stupid or a failure; it means we had the courage to try something new. That's something to be incredibly proud of. The most successful people in the world - the people who have achieved the greatest things - have failed a ton of times. They've had the courage to dream, and to try and try again; to put themselves out there and see what happened.

It's okay to let go of perfectionism. You don't have to be perfect for anyone else, and especially not for yourself. It's okay to make mistakes and fail a few times as you work towards something new. In fact, it'd be kinda' strange if you didn't. It's a natural and normal part of any experimentation or learning process. Think about babies, learning to walk. They fall down, they feel momentarily confused or discouraged, and then they try again. We don't shame them for not figuring it all out perfectly the first time. We don't give up on them. We know that every journey is different, and that each gorgeous bub will get there in their own sweet time.

I can't even begin to fathom how much stress and anxiety in my life has come from trying to be perfect. To say the perfect thing in an interview or on a date, or to wear something perfectly appropriate to an event. The daft thing was that this was all self-imposed. Ninety-nine percent of the time, no-one else cared. They were focused on the many things going on in their own lives. And if they *were* focused on me for some reason, the vast majority of them didn't want perfection; they wanted the real me. They wanted authenticity, like we all do.

So much of my constant striving for perfection was wrapped up in my lack of self-love. It was wrapped up in my willingness to be whatever I thought the other person wanted me to be. I was a chameleon because I didn't fully love and accept (or, let's face it, even really *understand*) the real me.

I was insecure and looked to other people for validation or approval, so was it any wonder I thought I needed to be perfect for them? I held myself to an impossible standard because I thought that was the way to win love.

The more I've released perfectionism, the happier I've become, and as a beautiful knock-on effect, the less I've expected perfection from others. Releasing perfectionism feels warm and open and real, after decades of strict rigidity. It feels like authenticity and love.

Years ago, I signed up for a yoga challenge that involved going to twenty classes in four weeks. Full disclosure here: I was hopeless at yoga at the time. Not only did I struggle to do most of the poses, but I also couldn't quite grasp what all the fuss was about. I didn't get it; why did people rave about their yoga practice? What was so amazing about stretching and breathing all over the place?

I was confused, but curious enough to find out.

In my first class, I felt like there was a huge flashing neon sign over my head screaming: *IMPOSTER!*

As I followed the instructor through the poses, I grew more and more frustrated and upset as I failed to do any one of them perfectly.

Leaving class that day, I was in a foul mood, wishing I'd never signed up for the stupid challenge in the first place, and seriously considering never setting a bare foot in a yoga studio ever again.

Thankfully, the following day I pulled myself together. Since I'd already paid for it, I figured I might as well give it another try. In class that day, I felt just as much of a failure, wobbling all over the place like an uncoordinated jellyfish while I imagined all my classmates silently judging and sniggering at me.

Class three wasn't much better, I'm afraid. But slowly over that week, I began to let go and focus more on feeling my way into the flow. I noticed tiny changes in my posture and breathing. I started thinking of my classmates as friends and imagined we were all on the same team (rather than me standing out like a sore thumb and feeling self-conscious that I didn't belong).

Once again, as I released my desperate need to be 'perfect', I began to relax and have more fun. And lo and behold, releasing my steely grip on results opened up more space to actually get better at the practice of yoga. By the end of the month, my posture had improved, I was sleeping more soundly, and I actually looked forward to every class.

Practice makes perfect, as they say, but it also creates a lightning rod for our backbone. Each time we break down a bigger goal into achievable stepping stones and complete each one, we feel good about ourselves. Taking action generates authentic confidence, and that confidence spurs us onto the next challenge. It's a beautiful snowball effect that keeps us growing ever outwards, slowly creating a life, and the confidence, we truly want.

I'll always remember the first time Dom and I were interviewed together, as joint partners in our business. Afterwards, my mind raced as I painstakingly went over every single word I'd said, whether I'd gotten my point across clearly, and all the tiny details I could have said and done differently.

I was so absorbed in this mental dissection of my responses that, at first, I barely even heard Dom say, "I think we did really well for our first time!"

As I turned to look at him, and his words slowly sunk in, it dawned on me how much pressure I always put on myself to get it right the first time. How little grace and wiggle room I left myself for simply practicing a new skill, without demanding that I exceed my every expectation.

My constant striving for instant perfection wasn't self-love; it was quite the opposite.

Whether we're talking work, relationships, health, or sobriety, it can be so tempting to be hard on ourselves and berate ourselves for not being further along on our journey. It can be so easy to forget the goalposts and milestones we've already achieved.

What if we let go of all the unrealistic expectations we put on ourselves, and approached something new as simply just 'practice'? Would we approach it with a lighter heart? With more joy and creativity?

I deeply suspect that if we went back and reviewed our history and recognised how far we've already come, we might just find ourselves celebrating our evolution, and feeling grateful for all the lessons we've experienced so far (even - or especially - the hard, messy ones!). We might just discover that practice and progress are a whole lot more beautiful and rewarding than perfection will ever be.

Being emotionally healthy and mature means putting more value on our growth than on the lofty heights of perfection. It means owning our mistakes and learning from them. It means giving yourself a chance to try, and fail, and try again.

Each failure is just one tiny blip in an ongoing journey of development. Each blunder makes you stronger than if you'd never tried. It's okay if new habits don't 'stick' the first time around. It's okay if we mess up, make mistakes, or don't always get it right. What matters most is what we do next.

So go ahead and practice. Give it your best shot. You have absolutely everything in the world to gain.

Here's to your growth.

18. Self Care is an Inside Job

They say 'wisdom' teeth are so named because they make an appearance much later, at an age where people are presumably more mature and 'wiser' than they were as a child.

Presumably.

I remember when one of mine made its presence first known. The year was 1999 and I was twenty-four years old. I'd been living in London for three months; long enough to find a job, but evidently not long enough to find myself adequate health care providers.

When a throbbing toothache woke me one morning, I gently brushed my teeth and went to work, hoping it would get better. It didn't. By lunchtime, I could barely stand the pain.

Asking my colleagues for recommendations, I started dialling dentists. Unfortunately, it seemed that every dentist in the area was fully booked. None of the clinics were accepting new patients; not even for an emergency appointment.

By the time I put the phone down after the eighth call, I was in tears. I told my boss I was leaving and went home to take painkillers.

When one of my flatmates (no doubt tired of listening to my pitiful whimpering) suggested washing the painkillers down with half a bottle of vodka, I thought it was a grand idea. *Anything* to stop the intense throbbing that felt like it was pounding itself into my skull.

Oh, I had teeth, alright. What I didn't have, it seemed, was even a lick of wisdom.

Thankfully, I woke up the next morning, although it wasn't pretty. Not only did I now have a hideous hangover, but my mouth was in even more agony. To my eternal relief and gratitude, another flatmate took pity on me and kindly bundled me up and took me to see her dentist.

After an eternity in the waiting room, her dentist finally agreed to see me. As I followed him into the treatment room and climbed onto the dentist's chair, the smell of antiseptic nauseated me.

Quickly inspecting the nasty little troublemaker that had set my jaw on fire, the dentist concluded that the tooth was 'impacted'. As I blinked at him, he explained the offending tooth was crookedly positioned and had effectively become trapped within my jaw, resulting in the infection that had brought my regular life and sanity to a screeching halt.

His professional opinion? Pulling the tooth right then and there.

Having always been terrified of dental work (no doubt exacerbated by having five teeth pulled in the chair in preparation for braces, on one very traumatic day when I was twelve), I managed a tearful "NO!" before I began sobbing again. The dentist sighed and reluctantly gave me a prescription for antibiotics and painkillers instead.

In the years that followed, numerous other dentists suggested pulling that tooth too, but no way was I having a bar of *that*, no thank you, sir. Nope, better to take medication, drink more vodka, and forget all about it. Clearly I was averse to conflict and its resolution, even within my own body.

You've guessed how this story ends, right?

At forty-one years of age, the clock finally ran out. I could hide from it no longer. All three of my wisdom teeth (I wasn't wise enough to warrant four, apparently) had to come out.

My surgery was booked for later that month.

I must admit, I freaked out for a day or so, before deciding *enough was enough*. There was nothing I could do about it; it was my destiny one way or another, so I may as well choose to feel *empowered* about it this time. Not a scared girl, giving her power away to booze and fear, but a wise woman, taking charge of her health -

and herself - for once and for all.

So I got busy. I stocked our fridge with a heap of ingredients for green smoothies, porridge, and a heap of other mushy meals. I loaded my phone with inspiring podcasts and videos; gathered up a pile of books I'd been meaning to read; and even picked out a few new TV shows to keep me occupied throughout the recovery.

As I busied myself with piling extra blankets and cushions onto the couch, it occurred to me that before I stopped drinking, I really didn't have very much experience with 'caring' for myself. I was much more of the school of thought that 'self-care' was boring, and you either went hard or went home (the insinuation being, of course, that I was much too tough to ever do the latter).

In one of my office jobs in Perth, I worked with a woman who totally intrigued me. About five years younger than me, she was always impeccably groomed. She was one of those rare creatures who seemed to have life all figured out. What fascinated me most was her air of quiet confidence and self-respect. If you offered her another drink or a slice of a deliciously gooey chocolate cake, she'd reply with a big smile, "No thanks, it's not good for me."

I found her equally baffling and awe-inspiring. I often wondered what she did in her spare time. What was her life like, if she never did anything that was bad for her? I couldn't imagine. None of my friends or family behaved that way, and I certainly didn't.

She reminded me of another woman who'd worked on my office floor when I lived in London. This woman wasn't classically beautiful, but she was always calm and well-spoken, and always looked exceptionally healthy and well groomed.

One morning, one of my co-workers was admiring this British vision of loveliness when another co-worker teasingly asked if he had a crush on her.

"Well, yeah," he said with a shrug. "She looks after herself."

As I swivelled my chair back to face my computer that day, his comment puzzled me. I didn't even realise that 'looking after yourself' was a quality that others found attractive. I'd always believed that simply flirting and showing the guys I could drink as much as them made me more attractive. I mean… *didn't it?*

I suspected there was a lesson in there somewhere, but try as I might, my confused little mind couldn't quite connect the dots.

I was still grappling to comprehend this many years later when, in the midst of the emotional chaos and all-consuming heartbreak that is divorce, a friend sat me down to give me some advice. Looking deep into my eyes, and taking my hands in hers, she said, "Bex, you need to be your own best friend through this."

Again, I was mystified. *Huh?* What did that even *mean?* I stared at her blankly and nodded as though I understood, but inside, I was terrified. So I did what I always did: I drank my fear away. I ate sugary treats for breakfast, skipped all other meals, racked up more credit card debt, spoke hatefully to myself, and shoved my feelings deep down, where I hoped I'd never have to find them.

The worst part was that the more I treated myself badly, the more I wanted to.

Learning to take better care of myself was a long and winding process. For me, sobriety was the key to my self-healing and to everything else. Sobriety was the first domino. All the ways I wanted to change and show up in the world sat behind that first domino. The health improvements; the relationship overhaul; the deep connection with others. They were all dependent on getting that first (ridiculously stubborn) little tile in place.

Your first domino could be as big and stubborn as an addiction to alcohol, smoking, shopping, or scrolling. Or it could be as significant as a single epiphany that you deserve to be treated better by *you*; the one and only person you will spend 24/7 with for your entire life.

I'd always believed that 'self-care' was simply about massages and bubble baths. To discover that, in actual fact, it was more about embracing my inner child and *parenting* myself, totally blew my mind.

The entire concept of real self-care was so foreign to me that, in early sobriety, one of my ruling mantras became: "Self-care is my number one priority right now." As I repeated this over and over, I started finishing work at a healthy time, avoiding overwhelm, and taking myself to bed early. I gave myself permission to feel my emotions (even when it was scary), to stop trying to be Wonder Woman and do it all, and to avoid people or places that triggered me, even if that meant backing out of events or declining invitations. I learnt how to take better care of my finances and establish healthy boundaries, and took responsibility for the people I surrounded myself with.

I wasn't always great at any of these things (especially the first time around), but each time I chose my longer-term health and happiness over what was immediately comfortable or easy, I got a little better at them.

The truth is, just like happiness, self-care is an inside job. No one can do this for us, and it's not always fun, easy, or simple. But as we learn better methods of self-care, we become happier, healthier people. When we're in touch with ourselves and our own feelings, we're more able to show love and compassion for others. When we're filling our own bodies and emotional tanks with self-respect and loving care, we in turn have much more to give to our families, friends, and the world at large.

Most importantly, we develop a deep sense of respect and love for ourselves. A love that is unshakeable. A love that is not dependent on the opinions or approval of others.

Ignoring my need for dental work wasn't self-love; it was neglect. Being a big baby about it and hoping it would all just go away wasn't the kind of advice I would give to - or the way I would parent - a child, so why was I doing this to myself?

So often in my work, women confide in me that they found it easy to stay sober when they were pregnant because they did it for the love of their baby. When they're no longer pregnant, they struggle to muster that same love for themselves. That's deeply unsettling when we stop to think about it, huh?

Have you ever looked at a photo of yourself at age three or four? If it's been a while, go take a peek now. Pull out that photo and look deeply into the eyes of that young child. Think about the hopes and dreams that existed behind those tiny eyes. How would you speak to that child every day? How would you protect, love and care for them? What kinds of hard decisions would you make on their behalf in order to ensure their long-term wellbeing?

What would you like to model for them about practicing self-kindness every day, and treating and speaking to themselves with love and compassion? What advice would you give them about not abandoning or betraying themselves in a misguided attempt to please others?

What kind of life and happiness would you ultimately want for them?

The truth is, that child still lives within you. That tiny tot still craves the same love, security, and safety. The empowering part is, now that you're an adult, you have the complete power to give it to them.

You might just find, as I did, that the more you ponder these questions, the better care you take of yourself. And funnily enough, in direct contrast to the downwards spiral of neglect and self-harm, the more you care for yourself, the more you want to.

At its core, through the journey of self-care, I learnt to be my own best friend. I developed a deep love and respect for myself. I was able to give more love to others, and I was able to finally create a life I truly love.

I wish all this for you, and more. Because love is always the answer.

19. Reclaiming Your Power

How many bad haircuts have you had in your life? If you're like most people, I'm guessing quite a few. One of my worst encounters took place when I was in my late-twenties and lived in Sydney. Sick of spending half my Saturday in the hairdresser's chair, I came up with the brilliant idea to sneak a quick haircut in on my lunch break. A short search online informed me that a salon very close to my work was offering special deals on midweek cuts. *Perfect!*

Momentarily forgetting that it's never a great idea to blindly traipse into a new salon that you have no experience with or recommendation for, I skipped down the street towards my appointment. A satisfied smile played on my lips as I imagined my chic new do and congratulated myself for being so savvy.

Oh, optimism. You kidder.

I arrived to find the salon deserted, but it looked clean and glamorous, so I figured it must just be an unusually quiet time.

"Hello?" I called out, still not seeing a soul. My voice echoed around the salon.

Suddenly a woman came flying around the corner. She looked to be in her thirties or so and appeared rather flustered.

"Hi! Hi," she said, waving her arms around and gesturing for me to take one of the chairs.

I did as she asked, and waited until our eyes met in the mirror before carefully and thoroughly explaining what I'd like (just a trim, with some slight, soft layering around the face).

"Great! Perfect. No worries," she said, making all the right sounds and gestures to signal we were entirely on the same page.

If you've ever had the misfortune to leave a salon in tears, I'm sure you can imagine the rest. Lulled into a false sense of security, I wasn't watching where the scissors were going as we chatted away happily. When she asked me to drop my head forward, I complied, fully trusting her kooky ways.

It was only as I saw a long strand of hair fall to the floor that the ringing started in my ears. Snapping my head back up, I gasped at the mirror. She'd lopped off all of the hair on my right side, from the point directly above my ear!

"What…?!" I exclaimed, my eyes practically

popping out of my head.

"Yes, that's right," she said, nodding and reaching back into my hair with her scissors. "Now I'm going to do this, see? It's a new style. It's good."

Frozen in utter horror, I watched her slice into the hair on the same side of my head, but even further back. *Was she trying to give me a mullet? Was this some kind of joke?*

"Stopppp!" I gasped, struggling to find the words. "No! I don't want... I... I still want to be able to tie it up!"

"Oh," she said, pausing for a moment before giving a slight shrug. "Well, I have to do the other side now, so it's even."

As I watched her raise her scissors to my left ear, my body went into meltdown. It was like being in one of those dreams where I couldn't scream or run or cry, no matter how hard I tried. In slow motion, I watched her cut the other side.

Standing back with a triumphant smile, she curiously avoided meeting my eyes in the mirror. "There! All done."

As I got up from the chair, I felt hot and dizzy and shaky. *Was I having an out of body experience?* Surely I was going to say something. Surely I wasn't going to actually *pay* for this atrocity?

But pay, I did. I even went so far as to nod dumbly when she handed me her card and said she'd see me next time.

I walked back to the office in a daze. *Maybe I was*

being overdramatic and no-one would even notice?

No such luck. I didn't even make it back to my desk before a coworker spotted me.

"Hey, nice 'do!" Alex from Accounting grinned.

That's all it took. Dropping my handbag, I sprinted towards the ladies bathroom. I barely made it inside before bursting into great heaving sobs.

I knew it! The cut was awful. I hated it, and I knew my boyfriend would hate it, and everyone in the entire world would laugh at me; the stupid girl with her stupid mullet haircut.

They didn't, of course. I cried frustrated tears in the shower the next morning when I realised yet again that half my hair was missing, but then I got creative with hair clips and up-do's and made the most of it for the next year or so until it grew back.

To be honest, I still don't know what I could have done to save the rest of my hair in that moment, other than telling that hairdresser exactly what I thought of her stupid 'new style' haircut, or running away before she could lop the other side. But I do know that when we feel disempowered, we're not our best selves.

Of course, a bad haircut is just one small, fleeting example, but whenever we feel powerless and violated and humiliated, it's extremely difficult to imagine we have any kind of autonomy over our lives at all.

I'm embarrassed to admit that I experienced another hairdresser like this many years later, and this time *I went to her more than once. Ohhh,* what's that they say about 'fool me twice…'?

This one gained my trust during the first few visits by, you know, acting like a normal human being. It was only on my fourth visit that she switched into some kind of zombie mode, hacking away at the back of my head like she was inciting revenge on an ex-boyfriend.

Appalled, but fairly certain it was just a momentary lapse of judgement, I told her I didn't like her new creation on my head *at all* and that I wanted my usual haircut next time, please and thank you (in twenty-eight flippin' weeks, when it would finally grow back!).

On my fifth visit, all was well. We were in perfect harmony again. Peace was restored to the galaxy.

My sixth visit was slightly better than the fourth, but still awful enough to see me bursting into tears the moment I got home.

On my seventh visit, the wheels well and truly came off. The zombie was back and she was out for blood.

When I arrived home afterwards in tears yet again, Dom exclaimed, "What are you *doing?* Why do you keep going back there? Go to a different one!"

"But I want her to be *good!*" I wailed, throwing myself onto the couch. "Her Instagram photos are good. She's good at doing everyone else's hair nicely. Why can't she be good at mine?"

"Because she's *not!*" Dom said, completely baffled at the insanity of my repeated behaviour.

He was right. I was stuck in a mess entirely of my own making. I was now at the stage of feeling Level

Ten Angst before every appointment. I dreaded going back there, and yet I was scared of trying a new hairdresser and having the same experience all over again.

I'd completely given my power away to zombie girl. I was forgetting that the next hairdresser might just blow my mind with how much better he or she could be. And even if the next one wasn't, I could keep trying again until I found a hairdresser I really gelled with. One that made me feel safe and happy, and look and feel my best.

The key was remembering that I always had a choice. Even the decision to do nothing (and keep coming home with a look that belonged in the early 1990's) was a choice.

This wasn't my only experience with giving my power away, and I'm guessing you have a multitude of examples of your own. Social media, for example, can be an intoxicating trap for our power.

The first time a coworker told me about Facebook, sometime in 2007, I scrunched up my nose.

"Sounds weird," I said. "Why wouldn't you just *email* your friends?"

Oh, I know. Famous last words. Over the next few years, along with droves of other people on the planet, I became increasingly addicted to those little likes and pokes and shares. I didn't yet own a smart phone, so I snuck glances at the website at work all day, and then hurried home to open it again on my laptop.

A couple of years later when I got my first iPhone, my obsession only escalated. Suddenly I could check for notifications at any minute of any day; and *ohhh,* how I did.

My then-husband and I often argued about my insistence on looking at my phone whether we were at the beach, out to dinner, or at a friend's house. "Put it away! You give too much energy to that thing!"

He was spot on the money, although I didn't realise it at the time, of course. Any addiction is first steeped in denial. I had a heap of drinking friends at the time and wanted to make them all laugh, so I felt compelled to post every day. Everywhere I went, I looked for the funniest picture I could take or the most amusing story or anecdote I could share. Rather than relaxing and simply enjoying my life, I was constantly (desperately) seeking connection through the screen.

All this checking and posting distracted me from noticing that deep down, I was lonely. I wasn't connecting with others in any real or meaningful way because I didn't really know myself yet, so I craved the endless approval and input of others. I gave my power away every time I posted, waiting with bated breath for the responses to come pinging in. Waiting for the dopamine hit that accompanied every notification that someone had replied. Someone cared. Someone thought I was funny.

And when they didn't? When a post was ignored? I was crushed. I felt like the event or moment I'd just shared had no meaning, even if I'd enjoyed it at the time. Every event, every experience, became tainted with wanting approval. My life, and all the events in it, no longer felt like my own.

Selling my soul for likes ultimately made me feel disempowered, just like those awful hairdresser visits.

When I finally realised this, it was an awakening. As I stopped posting on Facebook and began to actually relish my privacy, it was like I could see my life again for the first time. Suddenly I was doing things for *me* again, not for the amusement of other people. I noticed the deeper sense of connection and fulfilment that came with focusing more on calling, texting, and emailing my closest friends and family, rather than posting to hundreds of friends.

On the rare occasions when I did want to post something, I first checked in with myself and only posted if I was totally okay with the fact that it might be completely ignored. Was I posting to wish my expanded circle a happy New Year simply because it felt good, and wasn't really fussed about who saw it or didn't? Or would I feel bad if no-one replied? That is, was I posting it for *me*, or because I wanted validation?

Over the years, I took it even further. One night I was out to dinner with a friend when she was in the middle of explaining something.

"It's like…" she trailed off. Suddenly she clicked her fingers, and with a mischievous glint in her eye, said, "Quick! What's the first thing you did this morning?"

"Ooooh… Jumped in the shower!" I grinned, delighted. I loved silly guessing games.

"No!" she demanded, her face serious. "Try again. The first thing."

"Uummm," I furrowed my brow. "I thought about work."

"No! Bex! Come on! *The very first thing.*"

Now I was totally confused. I figured humour might help. With a cheeky grin, I tried again. "Uuhhh... scratched my butt?"

"No!" She said, exasperated, throwing her hands in the air before leaning in to give me the long-awaited answer. *"Checked your phone!"*

Bursting into laughter, I shook my head as I told her, "Oh no. No way. No phones in the bedroom, ever."

Her jaw almost hit the table as stared at me. *"What?!* Seriously? Well, you're the only one!"

"Yeah," I nodded, attempting to calm my giggles. "Because I've learnt that I don't function well if I do that."

In the past, I opened up my phone first thing in the morning, and before I'd even had a chance to wake up properly or focus on my life, I was absorbing other people's opinions and agendas. Being a sensitive soul, it affected me for the rest of the day.

That was, until I decided to take my power back and protect my energy. These days I let myself wake up, have a shower, have breakfast, and think about where *my* life is headed, before I consume anyone else's.

Of course, creating new boundaries isn't always easy. Back when I first declared my bedroom a phone-free zone, a friend continued to call late at night, growing increasingly upset when she couldn't reach me.

These were not emergency calls, mind you; she simply wanted to chat about random thoughts she'd had, or future plans she wanted to run by me.

One morning when I called her back, she exploded down the line. "Well, *finally! Why don't you ever answer your phone?!*"

"I do, hon," I calmly reminded her. "Just not between eight p.m. and eight a.m."

I can't even begin to tell you how liberating and empowering it felt to do what was best for me, even if it wasn't someone else's preference.

As people-pleasers, we tend to stay small or quiet, or bend to the will of others, in order to keep the peace or make everyone happy. Way too often, we sacrifice our voice in order to be agreeable. Is it any wonder then, that we feel inauthentic and suffer?

When I realised that even having all the social media apps constantly pinging my phone totally stressed me out, I disabled all notifications and put my phone onto silent. Now I can breathe. Now I'm living life based on my own personality and preferences.

Each day we step up and take control of our lives is another day we get to live life to its fullest, and reach our full potential.

The fact is, life will always be wild and full of unexpected twists and turns. We only ever have control of our own reactions and responses. By not giving our power away, we begin to develop a higher level of emotional maturity. We start to recognise that things in life are not happening 'to' us - they're happening 'for' us - so we can grow, evolve, and become all that we're meant to be.

This also means that when we're in a situation or conflict, rather than reacting and going bananas, we're better able to stop to consider: *What can I learn from this?* It's incredibly empowering to have the wisdom and wherewithal to be able to think: *What could I do differently here? How could this situation help me to grow?*

There's no doubt taking personal responsibility for your life is challenging. It takes courage to own your reactions, hold yourself accountable, and acknowledge when you've messed up. Choosing what's best for you in the face of what others want takes boldness.

But this is your one, precious life. You are the CEO of all of it. No-one's coming to do this for you; it's up to you to reclaim your power and choose to live in a way that feels liberating and authentic to you.

Be brave. Start small. Go within. Trust your heart, and rediscover what makes *you* happy (hint: it's not at the bottom of the bottle, or the result of someone else's behaviour, I promise).

The great news is, you already have everything you need, inside of you.

20. The Magic of Authenticity

I was forty-three years old the second time I walked down the aisle, which seems so peculiar to me, even as I type that out. I never imagined I'd *ever* be that age, and especially not on my *wedding* day. Despite the superficial fears of my thirty-one-year-old self, I had some wrinkles, sure. But you know what else I had? A healthy dollop of hard-won wisdom, emotional maturity, and life experience.

This time around, my motivation - the energy underpinning the entire day - couldn't have been more different. Before we got engaged, Dom and I had been together for six years and it didn't bother me in the slightest. I felt zero external or internal pressure to hurry things along, and couldn't give two hoots what anyone else thought. I wasn't fussed if we never got married. I was just happy to be with him - to choose each other every single day - and I felt like we had all the time in the world.

When we finally decided that we really did want to take our relationship to the next level, it was a completely natural progression built on open communication, full consciousness, and mutual respect. What other people might think didn't factor into the equation even one little bit.

I no longer feared that being unmarried meant I was unloveable, because we were both so at peace with who we were. We could see that we were two complete people coming together equally, rather than one half desperately hoping to be made whole. We challenged each other often, and we also weren't afraid to recognise or call ourselves out on our *own* preconceived notions or limiting beliefs.

Finding that special someone is amazing, and it's true, the right partner can certainly help us to heal in some ways, but that doesn't free us up from having to do the hard, messy, inner work. Being deeply devoted to this level of truth and integrity meant I created an internal sense of self-worth that was no longer based on what others think. I started to really know myself and my needs, goals, and values, as well as my triggers and areas of self-sabotage.

I knew that Dom and I wanted to continue to build a life and grow together, not because we were looking to be rescued or saved, and most definitely not because it was expected of us. And oh boy, did our wedding reflect this!

We got engaged amidst a flurry of love and excitement in April of 2018. We had no intention to rush into choosing a wedding date, thinking we'd probably wait until the following year. But purely by chance, in early August we heard that one of our favourite venues was hosting weddings for the very first time. This venue was not only special; it also held a significant place in the story of our relationship.

Once upon a time, when Dom and I were first dating, he took me to an outdoor cinema event at the university he'd graduated from years before. I'm not sure what I expected this venue to be like, exactly, but as we walked hand-in-hand around the faculty buildings, and through a large wooden gate into a hidden garden, I all but lost my mind. Suddenly we were surrounded by skyscraper-tall pine trees, lush ferns, and twinkling fairy lights. It was the most spellbinding place I'd ever seen.

"Oh my God!" I breathed, reaching out to squeeze his hand. "It's like the Ewok forest!"

In the years that followed, we developed a tradition of heading there to see the first movie of the year, gathering our friends together for a pre-film picnic to see in the New Year in style. No matter how many times we went there, I was always gobsmacked that any place could be so unexpectedly beautiful.

And now, for the very first time, they were offering

up this enchanted forest for a wedding venue.

There was just one teensy little catch. The space was used as an outdoor cinema throughout the Summer and was only available for weddings in the shoulder seasons. If we waited until next Autumn, a large marquee would be erected, designed to be used by all wedding parties for the entire season. Alternatively, if we wanted to go ahead and book for this Spring, we could dictate the size of the marquee, which meant we could choose a smaller, cosier one. *Oh, the temptation!*

There were still two dates available in October. As in, *two months* later. We were booked to fly to Scandinavia for the month of September. Which meant, all up, if we decided to go ahead with this wild and wonderful plan, we'd have about five weeks total of on-the-ground planning time.

Five weeks. To plan an entire wedding. Not a year; not five months. *Thirty-five days.*

We were thrilled with the idea. No long, drawn out wedding planning process. No losing sight of what we really wanted (since there wouldn't be time). Just straight-forward, simple decisions. A big, uncomplicated YES to a day that would feel truly magical. A day that was completely *us.* A celebration that was fully conscious, and even… dare I say it? An event that was alcohol-free.

Cue the screeching halt of a record needle scratch.

I know, I know. I mean… dry weddings, right? Who *does* that?

It was an ambitious plan, I'll give you that. But

since neither of us drank, it was fun for us to think about. It made sense that we wanted to celebrate with our friends and family while they were authentically themselves. But how would we ever pull it off?

As we let ourselves get swept up in this zany idea, we figured the key to hosting a successful alcohol-free event would be to schedule it at a time of day when people are less inclined to drink.

When I first heard about brunch weddings, my heart almost exploded with the sweet perfection of it. Just go ahead and search 'brunch wedding' on Pinterest and tell me those images don't inspire the warmest of fuzzies in you. The morning sunshine, fresh flowers, and fruit platters. The dainty teacups, mini waffles, and gorgeous little bomboniere packages filled with crossword puzzles and freshly ground coffee beans. *Scrumptious!*

Granted, if we were brave enough to embark on this kind of adventure (and we were!), our day was likely to start somewhere close to dawn, but there was something so enchanting about the magic of celebrating our love in the newness of morning.

As we researched the possibilities, another huge benefit of brunch weddings deeply appealed to the newly-discovered sensitive introvert in me: they generally take place over a shorter duration. Most weddings I'd attended had started with a ceremony at 3pm, only to finish up around midnight. That's *nine* long hours of socialising! *Phew.*

Getting more excited by the second, we decided on

a ceremony time of 9am, with a reception from just 10am to 1pm. Long enough to have a great time; short enough to leave on a (natural) high. *Heaven.*

We didn't know anyone who'd ever hosted a morning wedding (or an alcohol-free wedding, for that matter), but we weren't afraid to be unique, and we certainly weren't worried about fitting in with what was expected of a traditional bride and groom.

Much to my own surprise, I didn't even buy a single bridal magazine! I wanted our day to feel completely and one hundred percent like *us,* and besides looking at a few photos of inspiration online, I no longer felt the need to compare what we wanted with anyone else's dreams or decades-old traditions of how it 'should' be done.

Wisely, this time around, I not only asked my fiancé to help me (and actually let him!), but we also hired a team of incredible people to help us bring our vision to life. Our catering team loved the challenge of creating a delicious brunch wedding menu, and our stylist was totally onboard with helping us to enhance the dreamy environment.

The great part about this kind of absurd planning timeline is there's much less time for everyone involved (us included) to obsess over the details. The even greater part about it is that you get to practice crystal clear communication, upholding healthy boundaries, and conflict resolution skills, almost daily.

As anyone who has ever planned a wedding will tell you, it's not always easy to do any of these things.

Weddings tend to bring out some pretty big opinions and personalities, and it can be excruciating (especially for recovering people-pleasers) to stand your ground.

I did it anyway.

When friends offered to organise hen's and buck's parties and bridal showers for us, but it just wasn't something we were interested in, we gratefully but politely declined. When a friend asked if her and her hubby could stay with us in our tiny apartment, and I knew things would be stupidly busy in the lead up, I said no (but matched her with other friends so they could share a holiday house together). When a family member insisted that a wedding simply isn't a wedding without champagne for the toasts, we quickly and easily told her, "No thanks, we'll have sparkling apple juice for the toasts. There'll be no alcohol at our wedding."

Knowing that our highest priority was to remain true to ourselves and our own personalities and preferences, made it that much easier to say no to all the things we didn't want. I knew first-hand that people-pleasing or bending over backwards for the approval of others would only make us feel resentful, and that this day wasn't about bowing to the whims of others. It was about sharing our joy and love with them. They could have all the things they wanted at their own weddings; this was ours.

At it's core *(praise the heavens above),* I no longer needed anyone else's approval. I wanted everyone to have a great time, of course, but I also wanted this day to be incredibly special to me and Dom. I knew exactly what it was like to spend the first morning as a newly-wed sobbing in the shower, and this time, I wanted the complete opposite of that. I wanted to spend the next day utterly blissed out, knowing we'd put each other first.

As for the day itself, I only wish I could have captured the very essence and bottled it. To our sheer delight, we'd never seen bigger smiles on the faces of our loved ones.

Our stylist had decorated the clear marquee with fresh, whimsical flowers, tea light candles, and festoon lighting to add a warm glow, highlighting the soft morning light and the beauty of nature all around us.

When stating dress code on the invitations, we'd suggested 'garden party attire' and encouraged our friends and family to be themselves and have fun. As a result, we were greeted with a sea of dreamy pastel colours and glorious floral ties and dresses that truly added to the atmosphere.

We totally went to town with the catering, serving a breakfast course (mini quiches, waffles, chia pots and bruschetta), followed by a lunch course (tarts, sliders and arancini balls), before my favourite, the dessert course (choc brownies, lemon meringue tarts and carrot cake muffins). We sipped on specialty blend coffee, herbal tea, freshly squeezed orange juice, and sparkling apple juice. Our wedding cake was an incredible strawberries-and-cream 'cheesecake' made from cashews and other goodness. It was all so morning-appropriate and fantastically delicious.

Some things still went wrong, of course. But all the regular wedding hiccups didn't bother me the same way because my motivation and focus was different this time. All I cared about was that we were happy and in love, and celebrating our joy with our favourite people. Everything else was just fluffy details.

After Dom's speech, much to the amusement of everyone, I spontaneously grabbed the microphone and shared some words, straight from the heart, with absolutely zero plan. Releasing all thoughts of perfectionism, I remembered only that vulnerability and authenticity build intimacy. Our loved ones didn't want a speech I'd perfected a hundred times: they wanted truth and in-real-time magic. Or at least, that's what they got!

I'd never imagined how much fun - and how freeing - it could be, to socialise and *be* in the world as my true self.

I'll always remember a moment during the event when I realised that the entire marquee was buzzing. The atmosphere was electric. These gorgeous people were beaming and more jovial than I'd *ever* seen them before, at any party or otherwise. It was one of those true 'pinch me' moments.

Even more exciting was when, much to our surprise and joy, the vast majority jumped up to shake their booties on the dance floor - totally sober!

Dom and I were on cloud nine for days.

I'd experienced real connection, authenticity and intimacy, by embracing who I truly was. And I glowed with the knowledge that I hadn't betrayed myself one tiny bit. I'd come such a very long way.

I wish that for you too, angel. All of it. Not just in organising events that are important to you, but throughout your entire life.

You don't have to betray or abandon yourself in order to receive love from others. Your own love and approval is worth infinitely more than any you could ever receive from anyone else. It's the key to true confidence and self-worth.

Your integrity, honesty, and authenticity is a vast treasure chest of unexplored wonders that will help you create fulfilling relationships - and the life - you truly want.

As for the nay-sayers? They have their own life to live. This is *your* one precious experience on this remarkable planet.

Stay true to yourself, own your power, and make yourself proud.

ABOUT THE AUTHOR

Rebecca Weller is a Health and Life Coach, Author and Speaker. Named 'one of Perth's leading Health-pre-neurs' by The Sunday Times Magazine, Rebecca helps women from around the world to get their sparkle back and create a life they love.

Author of the bestselling memoir, *A Happier Hour*, the long-awaited follow-up, *Up All Day*, and her newest book, *Chameleon*, Rebecca writes about love, life, and the strength and potential of the human spirit.

Her work has been featured by the Telstra Business Awards, The Australian, The Huffington Post, Mind-BodyGreen, Fast Company, Good Health Magazine, Marie Claire Australia, and Elle Quebec.

Rebecca lives in sunny Perth, Western Australia, with her husband, Dominic.

Learn more, plus receive a weekly love note full of inspiration and special bonus gifts, at BexWeller.com.

OTHER BOOKS BY
REBECCA WELLER

A Happier Hour

What if the very thing you believed to be your biggest flaw and weakness, actually turned out to be your biggest gift?

When Rebecca Weller's pounding, dehydrated head woke her at 3am, yet again, she stared at the ceiling, wondering why the hell she kept doing this to herself.

At 39 years of age - and a Health Coach, no less - she knew better than to down several bottles of wine per week. Her increasingly dysfunctional relationship with alcohol had to stop, but after decades of social drinking, she was terrified of what that might mean.

How could she live a joyful existence, without alcohol? How would she relax, socialise, or celebrate - without wine?

In sheer frustration, on a morning filled with regret and tears, she embarks on a 3-month sobriety experiment that becomes a quest for self-discovery, and ultimately, transforms her entire world.

A Happier Hour is a heartfelt, moving, and inspiring true story for anyone who has ever had to give up something they loved in order to get what they truly wanted.

Find your copy at BexWeller.com/Books

Up All Day

One woman's journey to finish what she started…

In her bestselling memoir, *A Happier Hour*, Rebecca Weller shared her story of embracing an alcohol-free life with a steely determination to reach her true potential.

But as she celebrates her second year of sobriety, she's challenged to determine what that really means. With hangovers no longer holding her back – with eyes wide open and nowhere to hide – can she find the courage to confront her secret lifelong dream?

She's about to discover that her hard-won sober status will only take her so far. What comes next is up to her.

Up All Day is an uplifting story for anyone who has ever had to conquer themselves in order to conquer their dreams. Because it turns out the biggest battle we'll ever face in reaching our creative potential, is the one that takes place inside of all of us.

Find your copy at BexWeller.com/Books

Made in the USA
Middletown, DE
03 August 2021

45277420R00139